AIN'T NO **DUMMY** AROUND **HERE**

A story of finding my voice
and identity in God

DIANA A. NICHOLLS

AIN'T NO DUMMY AROUND HERE
A Story of Finding My Voice and Identity in God
Copyright © 2018
Diana A. Nicholls
ISBN 97897696139-0-4

All rights reserved. No part of this publication may be reproduced, stored in a retrieval system, or transmitted in any form or by any means – electronic, mechanical, digital, photocopy, recording, or any other – except for a brief quotation in printed reviews, without the prior permission of the author.

Unless otherwise indicated, all Scripture quotations are taken from the New King James Version, © Copyright 1982 by Thomas Nelson, Inc. Used by Permission. All rights reserved.

Please note that several actual names of persons and places mentioned in this book have been changed or omitted to protect the identity of the relevant parties.

Order copies of books or send requests for speaking engagements to dnicholls_1965@hotmail.com or call 246-425-3047 or 246-237-8934

Design and Printed by: Cole's Printery Ltd, Barbados

Dedicated to my four daughters Victoria, Christine, Crystal and Shelly-Ann, and to the late Reverend Dr. Louise Joseph who saw the eagle in me before I even knew I had wings.

Acknowledgements

I could not acknowledge anyone before giving all the glory to Almighty God, the Potter who has never left my side but has been faithfully working to complete that which He has started in me. After Him, I give due credit to my daughters Victoria, Shelly-Ann, Christine and Crystal who supported me in this project, and to my grandchildren. To all those close to me, including those dearly departed, who would have pushed me continually and encouraged me to believe in myself, who prayed and prophesied purpose into my life, I say a heartfelt Thank You. I especially acknowledge the late Dr. Joseph, past principal of Bethel Bible College of the Caribbean, my editor Ruth Moïsa and all those who worked to get this book from concept to publication, Apostle Jacqueline Cumberbatch, Dr. Anthony Cummins, my church family, friends and colleagues in the ministry.

About the Author

Apostle Diana A. Nicholls (nee King) was born in Barbados on October 11th, 1965. Privy to both the hardships and adventures of a poor, black child growing up in the West Indies during the sixties and seventies, her life was made all the more challenging by a severely delayed speech development. It was this that led her parents to discover that Diana was born with a speech disability. With ten other children to clothe and feed, they could not afford to redirect additional time or resources to helping Diana overcome this disability which still affects her today.

Diana fought her way through life with the help of mercy angels sent by God. She surpassed the expectations of others to graduate from primary school, secondary school and years later, Bible College. God would later reveal to her why His hand was upon her life. She was to be His hand-maiden. Juggling the responsibilities of family life, Diana followed the prompting of God on her heart to serve Him and His Church. From church janitor and secretary, to Youth President and Evangelist, Apostle Diana A. Nicholls now pastors the United Family of Praise In Christ Mission Assembly, located in Barbados. She powerfully preaches the word of God across the Caribbean and amazingly, it is only when she preaches, that she is able to speak without her heavy stutter. She is mother to four beautiful daughters and delights in helping them raise their own children in the fear of the Lord.

Contents

Part One – *'Dummy' Diana and the Village Years*
Chapter 1 – *Dummy Diana* 3
Chapter 2 – *Meeting Jesus* 7
Chapter 3 – *Mrs. Drakes* 10
Chapter 4 – *My Mother* 15
Chapter 5 – *Child-like Faith* 21
Chapter 6 – *Becoming Adventist* 26
Chapter 7 – *First Love's Bite* 30

Part Two – *God in the Valley*
Chapter 8 – *Gi' Me Back Me Chile* 39
Chapter 9 – *Double Delight* 43
Chapter 10 – *Tied Up in a Knot* 47
Chapter 11 – *Mr. Codrington* 49
Chapter 12 – *Baby Steps in Christian Service* 53
Chapter 13 – *Encounters with the Holy Spirit* 56
Chapter 14 – *Health Scares* 61
Chapter 15 – *Two Pigs and a Visa* 64
Chapter 16 – *Cut Down* 68
Chapter 17 – *A Lump and a Leg* 73
Chapter 18 – *Divine Healing* 81

Part Three – *Accepting the Call*
Chapter 19 – *Jackson Nazarene* 87
Chapter 20 – *Favor at NCC* 91
Chapter 21 – *Dirty Hands* 95
Chapter 22 – *Evangelist Nicholls* 103
Chapter 23 – *I've Made My Decision* 107
Chapter 24 – *House Divided* 112
Chapter 25 – *Call to the Pastoral Ministry* 116
Chapter 26 – *United Family of Praise* 124

Part One
Dummy Diana and the Village Years

Chapter 1
Dummy Diana

A child born in the east. That was me. October 11th 1965, one year before little Barbados gained her independence from Great Britain. I was born in the seaside village of Belleplaine, St. Andrew, on the rugged eastern side of the most easterly of Caribbean islands, where the deep blue waters of the Atlantic Ocean would crash the shores. I was born Diana King, fourth child to Keith Philips the bus-driver and Velda Philips née King, the home-maker, mid-wife and cane-cutter. I was born one of eight children from that union. My mother had three children from previous relationships and my dad fathered several outside of the marriage, some acknowledged, some only assumed because of an uncanny resemblance they bore to the rest of the siblings.

With so many children around - the norm for Barbadian families in those years. It was easy to get overlooked or pushed aside. In those days you had to have something that made you stand out in order to get noticed. You had to be a *Mary* with the pretty long hair, or a *John* with the really bad bow-legs, a *Susan* with fair skin and buck teeth. Even a David would get much attention, if he had a twisted hand from birth because somebody "wuk something" on either one of his parents.

As for me, I was Diana. To many, I was *Dummy Diana*, because I was the Diana that could not talk. It wasn't that I could not talk, but the words took so long to come out that if you waited for me to speak, you might miss your bus or burn the food on the stove or fall asleep. And with all the children my parents had, they scarcely had time to wait for me to get out what I wanted to say. When the words eventually did come out, I stuttered. Each syllable felt like a fifty-pound crocus bag of sugar being dragged from my lungs, the bag's fibers scratching along the back of my throat and making me gag. Trying to talk felt like just too much of an effort. I got noticed alright. But I wish I hadn't because I never felt like love and affection came with that notice.

My earliest memories of insults and abuse were at four years old. My siblings, two of my older sisters in particular, would tease me, even beat me up. "Dat is why yuh can't talk, yuh dummy!" they would say to me. "Who could blame them?" I thought. Who would want a dummy Diana in their family? The children in the community were worse with their taunts. They laughed at me and I had the most brilliant of insults to lash back - I was smart, really good at quick thinking - but when my come-backs came out of my mouth the children would laugh even harder at me.

In Belleplaine, the houses were no different from the typical chattel houses of the day. The house I was born in had three rooms, a bedroom for my parents, a bedroom for us children, and another room that had a table and a chair. My mother cooked in the yard on wood fire. The toilet was also outside. We had no running water. The bath was wherever you felt like taking one at the time - in the yard, by the community stand-pipe or in a public bath in the neighboring community of Shorey Village. We used the latter when we visited our maternal grandmother. We slept on a grass bed in my early years before my mother was able to secure a mattress for us.

My mother worked on a colonial plantation planting canes and vegetables. My father was a driver. He drove an ice-cream van and after that, a sand truck. Later he worked for the Transport Board as a bus-driver.

We were poor. But thankfully we had the majestic hillsides and stretches of green plains which drape across the eastern side of the island. These were my playing grounds as a young child, or sometimes my hide-away if my friends and I decided to carry away someone's yard fowl to kill it, cook it and eat it without being caught. In the early 60s, very few rural homes had a television or even a radio, so there was nothing much at home to keep us children entertained. We found that entertainment in the outdoors, in the streets under the watchful eye of some elderly person sitting at their front window, or we might venture over to a neighbor who had a television, stand by their door and peer in until they got weary of our presence and shooed us away.

There was a man who lived next door to us by the name of Mr. Alleyne. He was in his late 50s and had a serious disposition, probably caused by his years living in England before returning home to take care of his ailing mother. His house was next to the street light under which we children would play and talk… so he picked up on our conversations.

When the children called me *Dummy Diana* and hurled all types of insults at me, I would get mad and want to beat them up. Mr. Alleyne would call me over and tell me not to let them get under my skin. I remember him saying to me, "You are strong" and "God loves you". He had no children of his own but would look after the neighborhood children. He never believed in putting down persons or in fighting with each other. He would sit down by the window and talk to the children as they passed by. As he watched me growing up with all the children insulting me, he would shout out to me, "Diana, listen, you will grow into a fine lady. Hold your head high and take care of yourself and be who God wants you to be."

I would ask myself what he saw in me that was so special. And why could my family not see it too? I had many questions. But no one seemed to give me answers. And what about this God? What was it He wanted me to be and why did it have to include being a dummy?

Chapter 2
Meeting Jesus

In the 60s and early 70s, Barbados was still a very God-fearing, religious country. It didn't matter if you spent all of your time in a rum-shop, or if you were shacking up with a man who had fathered several children in the village, or if you were somebody's mistress. It didn't matter if you could not read nor write your name. You had an understanding that the sun rose and set because God decided it to be so and that if you prayed really hard for something and God heard, He would give you a miracle. There was a church on every street corner and even if your parents did not go a particular Sunday or Sabbath, they would send you to make sure you got the fear of God preached into you.

That is how I came to hear about this God. My parents sent me to St. Andrew's Anglican Church on most Sundays. The Church had such an extensive reach into the community that it seemed like the only place to be on Sundays for many people. I never saw my dad set foot in a church, not even to this day; my mother attended sometimes. Her mother was the famous Evangelist King from Shorey Village, a half-white woman with long hair. She was a Pentecostal. At that time, there was a Pentecostal church on every street and sometimes, you may have found two, three, even four different churches on one street.

God did not seem to speak much to me in the Anglican Church, but He seemed to have a lot to say in the smaller Pentecostal churches, which dotted our communities. Even though we would laugh as children among ourselves at what we saw, our young minds still had a sense that God was sacred and our approach to Him needed to be sacred as well. I remember attending a church on the main road and this old man came into the church. It might have been the pastor. At the time of his arrival there was a woman singing on the platform. She must not have been doing something right, though I did not notice what her mishap could be. Still, the Pastor rebuked her and all of a sudden, she dropped to the floor and began to roll about, hollering. There was talk among the older folks about demons. We used to laugh, but it made me know that this God was real.

I think I began to hear Him in the many revivals the smaller churches would have. "Revival" services were held in the open air; they were evangelistic in nature. Preachers would cry out that God was calling the backslider home and that people were to repent from their wickedness and turn to their Lord and Savior Jesus Christ, or face for all eternity hell's fire. Pastor Campbell, was a prominent female preacher in St. Andrew known for holding revivals at that time. People would be singing and dancing, crying and stomping. They would commit themselves to God, or go up to the altar to pray for a miracle. Sometimes the preacher would prophesy to people, and tell them about some wrongdoing in their lives that they needed to fix in order to get right with God. But many nights it was as if the songs themselves drew people to a place of conviction and desire to surrender their lives over to a Higher Being.

One night I remember standing at the back of the crowd, listening to this song being repeated over and over again:

> *Trust and obey, for there's no other way to*
> *be happy in Jesus, but to trust and obey.*

This song was a seed planted in my heart. Though I did not understand what it meant at the time, it would remain with me through many difficult moments in life I would later endure.

I don't recall that single defining moment this Jesus became a friend to me. However, I remember him being the comfort I so needed when the insults from friends and family hurt me deeply. I was told that God sent His Son Jesus to love me and save me. That made me love Him with all my heart because I wanted to be saved from my troubles. I would always pray in my own way to Jesus, asking him to help me to talk plainly, since I saw this as the source of all my troubles and since He was in the business of healing people. I had heard about Jesus being able to heal the blind, the deaf and the mute. And though I was not mute, I really needed Jesus to heal my speech disability. I believed with all my heart He could do it.

But the healing never came.

Chapter 3
Mrs. Drakes

The year 1974 was the first of many defining years for me.

It was the year when something happened to me, something so significant that I felt my years in the backside of the desert were finally over and I would finally have a chance to break through the ceiling of ignorance and poverty that hung over my family and many other families.

I was nine years old when an elderly Christian woman by the name of Mrs. Drakes approached my mother and asked her to allow one of her daughters to come live with her. The lady, a Pastor, was a respectable woman in the community. My mother brought the proposition to us children and asked us who wanted to leave home to live with the lady Mrs. Drakes. Both my hands shot up in the air with a speed that made my mother's eyes open wide. What was even more surprising was how quickly my heavy tongue was able to cooperate with my mind, at this stage wild with excitement. I blurted out, "Let me, let me go!" I so much believed that if I got the chance to go to Mrs. Drakes' house, my life would change and I would become better than my sisters and brothers. I felt no guilt wishing this, after years of being put down by them.

Mrs. Drakes lived in Welchman Hall, St. Thomas, the parish adjoining St. Andrew to the south. I loved her from the first time I met her. God had not healed my speaking but this woman was surely a miracle from God. Seeing her and knowing that she would take me into her home made my spirit do cart wheels. "Yea, I will grow better than my sisters and brothers", I told myself. "I'm going to have everything I always wanted. My own bedroom, my own clothes, shoes and everything I need. No more hand-me-downs, no more hunger, everything nice as spice!"

When I saw the house I would be living in, so big and pretty, I could not believe my fortune, I felt like a princess rescued. Yes, my life would be better than those who called me *Dummy Diana*.

The first few months with my adopted mother were awesome. In fact, her entire family was very loving and that made me happy. The home environment was far removed from what had been my normal. No one was insulting me and that in itself helped me to be more at ease and more confident when attempting to express myself. Mrs. Drakes believed that God could change me into a new person and my linguistic ability would not be the same. She saw me not only as a child, but also as a soul in need of salvation. I marveled at her remarkable patience with me. She would call me into her room and bid me to sit down in front of her. She would instruct me on how to pronounce words and she would make me read Psalms 23 aloud. To this day, I can recite this psalm plainly because of her drilling me at nine years old. But in other speaking exercises, progress was minimal. She would say to me, "Diana, now look at my mouth and repeat after me."

I tried many times but my slow speaking would remain.

There is an old Barbadian proverb which says, "Come see muh ain't come live with muh" (come see me is not come live with me), which means people usually put on a show when you visit them or stay with them as a guest, but if you stay long enough you will get to see their true colors. This was the case with me. Although Mrs. Drakes continued to be affectionate toward me, it was clear that her children saw me more like a home-help to be seen and not heard, as opposed to being part of the family. Mrs. Drakes had a daughter who was in her 50s at the time. She did not approve of my presence there and made it her business to let me know that by the way she treated me. As Mrs. Drakes was an old woman, my care fell mostly to her children. Many Sundays, the daughter would send me to Sunday school without breakfast. I loved Sunday school but having to sit through a church service hungry always made me feel like I would faint.

One Sunday, I decided to hide away and return to the house so I could eat all of the food that was prepared for me to have after church. When the daughter realized what I had done, she decided to give me no more food. I was ordered to go into the farm grounds after church to feed the pigs and pull vines for the rabbits to eat.

Mrs. Drakes' daughter had a shop in the basement of the family house. I began to watch and wait for her to turn her back so that I could take up biscuits, cheese and drinks. I would wrap them up in a bag and head across to the farm grounds to gather vines for the rabbits and partake of my stolen food.

Even in those moments of hardship, I sensed a divine presence in my life. I recall journeying through a neighborhood cane field one day. As I was walking, I saw a grave with a stone marked 1840 and that became my resting place. There, I would brace myself against the stone and cry out to God for help. The family I so wanted to get away from now seemed better than the situation I now found myself. Every time I saw my mother, I would tell her what was happening to me and that I wanted to return home. But she never believed me or rather, she ignored me because with me gone it was one less mouth to feed.

I stayed with the Drakes family for two years. Many days I was ill-treated by some family members. One of the adult grandsons in particular attempted to molest me on several occasions when I was outside feeding the pigs, but I would always find a way to escape him. I told my mother and Mrs. Drakes but nothing much came of my complaints.

In the darkest times, Jesus protected me. Psalms 23, which I had memorized by now, was a burning lamp within my mind and heart. Every morning I was always the first to wake from my bed and that allowed me to find something to eat. Some mornings I would go behind the house to search under a mango tree to see if I could find any mangoes that had fallen to the ground. One blessed morning, I ran under the tree and I found a big mango, my heart began to rejoice over this mango. It was so big and pretty that in my heart, I believed this mango had dropped from the top of the tree just for me. I didn't wash it, only wiped it off with my clothes and gave it a big bite. I never felt so frightened or sick in my entire life. As I bit the mango, I saw that there was a millipede in it. I began to cry for someone to come help me. My stomach was so upset from that mango. When I looked up to the house, standing at the bedroom window was Mrs. Drakes' daughter. She was looking at me and laughing. I never ate a mango again after that day until I became a woman.

Chapter 4
My Mother

My mother was my biggest challenge. Many of my insecurities as a young girl and growing into womanhood can be traced back to the relationship I had with my mother. My mother had no formal education so this was not something she pushed for her children to achieve. Her "education" was passed down to her from the women before her… and from what my father told her was expected of her as a wife. She was what you would call an "eye-catcher" in her youthful days. Even with three children already, her fair, smooth skin, curvy shape and long, soft hair was enough to catch the eyes of my father. Like many of the women in rural Barbados back then, my mother was poor but proud. She made it her business to keep the house and her children clean. She cooked for the family and frowned upon her children begging. She was an obedient wife to my father – to the point of old-fashioned subservience - and worked hard to help supplement his income by cooking for weddings, delivering babies and raising the eight children she bore for him. Her first three children lived with other family members because my father declared he was not putting a roof over another man's children.

I suppose my mother simply did not have time for a special needs child. My mother did not have time to motivate me in my earliest years of learning. If I took too long to call a word, she would shout at me, "Look girl, move from in front me and go learn to talk!" My delayed and impaired speech that could affect my education was not such a big deal to her. I don't remember her sitting down and talking to me seriously about anything. She showed us no affection in the form of hugs and kisses. We heard no "I love you", no "You are beautiful", no "Diana, you are special". Even to this day, when I tell her that I love her, she responds only with a "hmm". She accepted a whole lot from my father and from the perceived ideology of what a woman was supposed to be at that time. I remember the times my mother would get home late from working, maybe cooking for a wedding. She would come home to meet the door locked. My father would shout at her for coming home late and she would be there at the door whining and begging like a puppy to come inside. My older sisters were more forceful and would demand that the door be opened. Sometimes, when my father was not looking I would open the door for her and sneak back into bed.

When my menstrual cycle came, it was only by the grace of God, in the form of advice from a caring neighbor that I even knew what it was. My mother never sat me down as a young girl to teach me and prepare me for the changes I would soon experience in my body. When I told her about the arrival of my first menstrual cycle, she snapped at me and ordered me to go into the bedroom to retrieve some old piece of cloth because she had no money to buy any sanitary napkins. And that was that about my journey into womanhood.

For a long while, I was angry with my mother. Not the type of anger to disrespect her, but the type of anger that made me not want to be like her. In my eyes, I saw in her a woman who was very strong and resourceful. With 11 children, she had to be. She worked multiple jobs while managing a large family. I can still remember her delivering babies throughout the neighborhood. At times I would sneak away to whatever house she was at, peep through the holes in the wall (you were always sure to find a hole) just in time to see my mother pulling out the babies, and slapping them on their buttocks until they cried. Then she would cut the umbilical cord.

She also took up things from inside the home to give to persons in need within the community. She was in many ways more caring for the community than for us her children. But I felt in my young mind that my mother was also weak. She took and took and took, believing that her deliverance was in everyone else's hands but her own; in her husband's hands or in her children's hands, should they get the opportunity to live overseas to make better for themselves and the family. In my eyes, she did not take her own fate into her hands. And looking back, I see that it was mostly because of her that I fought so hard to rise from the dust of my existence.

One bank holiday, when I was still living at the Drakes house, my mother's family church had a picnic and I was able to go with them. I went to the picnic and rejoiced, hoping that when the picnic was over, my mother would let me sleep in Belleplaine and return to Welchman Hall in the morning. But this was not so. When the bus reached St. Thomas, my mother pressed the bell in the bus in order to put me out at the family of Mrs. Drakes.

I began to cry and cry, but this didn't move my mother, sisters or brothers. There were all in the bus laughing at me. My heart was so broken in pieces. I began to cry out harder and louder, so everybody could hear me. Mrs. Drakes came out from her house and asked me what was wrong. I said, "I want to go home and come back in the morning". No one listened to me. Mrs. Drakes began to hold my hands and pulled me in the house. While I was shouting and crying, she was still pushing me. I decided to push her off me and she fell to the ground. Her family came out and began to beat me with their hands. They shouted at me to leave their house. By then, the bus had already gone on, so one of Mrs. Drakes' grandson gave me 75 cents to catch the next bus to go home. I took the money from his hand, threw it at him and began to cry again. As I was sitting next to the road, he came, gave me the bus fare and said, "The bus is coming up the road, take the bus-fare and go home." I took it and stopped the bus.

I did not know where to press the bell for the bus stop nearest to my home so I decided to press it ahead of every stop. The driver asked me if I did not know where I lived. I told him I did but that I did not know the actual location of the bus stop. He replied, "Don't press the bell anymore. As soon as I reach

Belleplaine, St. Andrew I will let you know. I sat and looked through the window hoping he would not forget me.

As soon as he reached my village, he said to me, "Show me the gap where you live." I showed him and he stopped the bus for me to disembark. I was so happy to know I was back at home. I skipped and ran, skipped and ran up the gap. When I reached close to my house, I saw my mother and her friend sitting at the side of the road. The other woman shouted, "Velda, isn't that Diana running towards us?" I heard my mother reply, "No, it is not her. I put her at Mrs. Drakes in Welchman Hall, St. Thomas". I ran and shouted, "Mummy, I'm home." My mother jumped up from her seat with such a speed, as if someone threw ice down her back. She shouted at me, "How you got down here? I put you home; how you get here?" I told her the entire story but my mother refused to listen to me. She shouted at me, "Go into the house, when I come, I'm going to beat you so bad!"

Five minutes later, my mother came inside the house and shouted, "Bring me a stick, I'm going to beat her so bad!" I was never so frightened in my life. My mother was so mad, she said to my eldest sister, "Hold her! Hold her!" They held me down and my mother sat on me and began to beat me up so badly, that the stick struck me across my eyes and tore into my skin. I begged my mother to stop beating me, but she did not until she realized I was not breathing well. As soon as my mother got up from on top of me, I ran outside the house.

After a while, my daddy came home and saw me outside crying. When I told him what had happened, he turned to my mother and said, "If I was home, you would never beat she up; how you could do that to your child? If she wanted to come home, why you leave her?"

My dad told her that every evening, he saw me going into a field with a cutlass to cut grass. "And all your other children at home. How you could do that to Diana?" he asked her. My father took me in the house and ordered me to go to bed. My mother did not speak to me for three days, after which she declared she would take me back to Mrs. Drakes. I begged her, "No please, no!" She did not budge but took me the next day to apologize to Mrs. Drakes and beg her to take me back. When the family refused to take me back in – to my great satisfaction - my mother remained angry with me for days and always tried to remind me that if I was still at Mrs. Drakes' house, I would have been able to migrate to England and have everything I wanted. She also told me that she had too many children and couldn't handle raising anymore. My mother did not understand the pains and the hurt I was receiving and so the insulting began again. "That's why you can't talk; you will never be no-body," she would frown up her face at me and say. That hurt and hurt me. I felt like dirt. Like I and the dirt on the old wooden floor were one.

Chapter 5
Child-like Faith

Somehow, the oppression I faced in those early years never made me wallow in self-pity for too long. I had a fighter spirit in me and I resolved once more to prove to my family that I would become somebody. Looking back, I am convinced that God placed that resilience in me. I trusted Him in the best way I knew how to as a child and He continued to place people in my life who believed I was worth it, that I would be somebody. One such person was my primary school teacher, Margaret Connell. Ms. Connell always seemed to have extra faith in me. In fact, she was a woman of extras. She was extra tall and had two extra fingers, one on each hand. And she was extra patient with me. She was the first teacher I had and when I wanted to say something but struggled to do so, I would pull on the edges of her dress and squeeze the extra finger on one of her hands until the words came out of my mouth. She spoke with a posh dialect. She was direct but tender. She would always say to me that I was special and that she had a strong belief that I would make it in life. It was her faith in God that helped me to move from one level to the next in school, that and the encouragement I received from my childhood friend Shirley Vaughn. My friend Shirley Vaughn was truly a friend to me as a little girl. I might have beat loyalty out of her at the start of our friendship because she was one of the many that would fret me and call me *Dummy Diana*… but she turned out to be a really good friend. She would help me and teach me how to read and call words. She'd always say to me that I must take my time and talk but the words were still hard to get out. I had to say it eight times before I could call one word plainly.

The next-door neighbors, the Douglins who had moved to Barbados from England in the early 70s, had started to take a keen interest in me. They were Seventh-day Adventists who would go on to play one of the most pivotal roles in my walk with Jesus. This family led me to accepting Jesus as my Lord and Savior.

They not only showed an interest in the salvation of my soul, but in my education. Mrs. Douglin was the one that would sit me down and talk to me about God, and about my body, as I was becoming a young woman. Her three daughters embraced me as a sister and they were the ones who would help me with my schoolwork. I remember coming home with homework on afternoons and running over to their home, sitting on the floor and receiving assistance.

In 1976, it was my turn to sit the Common Entrance Examination. It still exists today and is a school-leaving examination in Mathematics and English that allows students – if they score enough marks – to be allocated to a secondary school based on grade and in part, on geographical zone. Several of my older siblings did not go to school beyond 11 years. In the 50s and 60s, girls would usually go to school until that age. Your education could be extended if you showed some remarkable academic ability to secure one of the scarce scholarships provided by government or some benefactor. Or you may have had parents with financial means. Barring that, you usually stayed home and cleaned the house until 13 or 14 when someone would employ you. You might get a job cleaning or working in a shop. Or, you might be taken on as an apprentice to learn how to cook and clean for a middle-class or upper-class family, or sew clothes, or God would smile down on you and a family might take you back to England with them, which is what my mother had hoped would happen to me.

I knew the odds were not in my favor. If my older siblings did not pass this exam, what chance could I have? I could not speak as well as they could and they tried to discourage me by saying *Dummy* would fail.

But on the morning of the exam, I had hope. I got up and forgot about all the discouraging words. God believed in me and my teacher said I could do it.

I got ready for school early in that morning and arrived there well before the starting time of the exam. As my classmates arrived, happiness was evident on their faces. They boasted amongst themselves of how well they would do and the schools they would be attending in the new school year. I remained sitting in a corner by myself and I kept my mouth shut. Most of the teachers believed in their hearts I would not pass my exam, but I had confidence in myself that I could do it.

While sitting in the examination room, I heard the voice of God say clearly to me, "Let not your heart be troubled" and the chorus of the song I had first heard years before at a revival came back to me.

> *Trust and obey, for there's no other way to*
> *be happy in Jesus, but to trust and obey.*

When I heard this voice I knew that God had sent my guardian angel to watch over me. I began to write. Sometimes I wrote things I did not understand but I had a strange sense it was God guiding me in what to put down on my paper.

After the examination, the children all went home. As soon as I reached home, my sisters laughed at me saying, "You do so bad, wait and see. You ain't going to no school you wait and see, you will be just like us." I did not listen to them. Instead, every day I awaited the results. The days could not come and go quickly enough for me. Then, finally, the results were back and the news spread like wildfire throughout the community. All of the children that sat the exam had to meet in the school hall for their results. I went in and sat very patiently, looking in the direction of my teacher who held the paper slips in her hand. The various teachers began to call out the names of the students and the school that they would be attending in the new school year. They began with the top schools first: Harrison College, Queens College, St. Michael's, Combermere…. I knew I was not in that class of students, but my ears were still open for my name.

Five minutes later, I heard my name called; Diana King - St. Leonard's Secondary School with a B in composition. I ran up to the teacher and took my results slip from her hand, laughing and shouting; "I have made it, thank you Jesus!" The teachers and students clapped for me. In that moment, I felt as if all of heaven's angels were standing up clapping for me and singing, "Diana, you have made it, we know you would have made it." I could not wait for the school bell to ring. When it finally did, I ran all the way to my gap, not stopping until I reached home. I kept shouting, "I passed, I'm going to a high school!" My sisters were shocked. They could not believe, after all they told me, that I would actually pass the exam! My mother took the slip from my hand and looked at it. She smiled and said, "Good". Her affirmation was like a hug to me. My daddy was also very pleased. I could not stop myself from smiling. My face was beaming and my heart was singing. God came through for me and proved to me that He was trustworthy.

Chapter 6
Becoming Adventist

I continued trusting God more in my life. As I began my first year at high school, I was placed in the highest form, but unfortunately, I was not able to remain in that class because I had no one to help me at home. The second term I was placed in a lower form to enable me to better cope with the schoolwork requirements. My adolescent years were now upon me and with the physical changes my body was undergoing, as well as a need to fit in more with my peers, I became overwhelmed. The Douglin family continued to work with me; they encouraged me and pointed me to a deeper relationship with Jesus. They invited my sisters and me to join their church and to receive baptism. I was taught how to seek the Lord while He was near. I heard the Pastor preach one day, "You're not too young to give your life to God, you're not too young to die."

That same year I was baptized at the Adventist Church. My life began to change; I began to hold fast to the life-style of the Adventists: not eating pork; not drinking Coke; not wearing any make-up or jewelry; and being serious about my faith. I began this new life as an Adventist, and so did my sisters and friends.

Adopting a more serious approach to life did have its advantages for us children. For me, my schoolwork became easier to understand. But there were also disadvantages in our mind. We began to feel like we were missing fun teenage activities.

There was a school fair at the Alleyne School in St. Andrew and all of the girls that were baptized at the Adventist Church, decided to go to the fair. Now the annual Alleyne School fair was no ordinary event. This was an event that everyone in the community looked forward to attending. Children were fussy about getting something new to wear to this fair. Adults came up with all sorts of things to sell - food, books, plants, household items and clothing. And who could forget the lucky-dip? One for girls and one for boys. That Saturday afternoon, we attended the fair, wearing the only thing acceptable to be worn at a school fair, the shortest pants we could find and a multi-colored halter top. So it wasn't that hard for our pastor to spot us as we passed the church, which faced the school grounds. Later that day, we were told that he was extremely upset and that as baptized Adventists we should have known we were not permitted to attend fairs. Having gone to the same fair for as long as we could remember, it never occurred to us that it was anything other than a highly anticipated community event. The next day we went to church, the pastor suspended all of us who went to the fair. We were not permitted to participate in any of the children's or church's activities. We could not even partake in the refreshments provided for the children. It did not take long for us girls to lose interest. We felt unwanted and so we turned our focus to the things and persons that made us feel otherwise.

And what about my friendship with Jesus that I treasured during my earliest years? I felt as if He had pulled away from me. He had to have done that, because I felt rejected by my own church family. Even my mercy angels, the Douglin family, seemed in my young mind to have distanced themselves from me, the wayward child who really just wanted to fit in with the other girls in the neighborhood.

Less and less, I sensed God's guidance like I did as a little girl. More and more the sound of silence lashed me in my face when I tried to connect with Him. I became aggressive, always ready for a fight. I had no friends with whom I felt I could talk. Mummy and daddy morphed into strangers from another planet. We spoke completely different languages. They were unable, in my young mind, to understand how I felt and where I wanted to go. I even feared God was done loving me. A voice kept telling me that He was done with me. He no longer loved me because I could not meet His standard. So I began to open myself to others whose standards weren't as high.

John came into my life soon after. He was a temporary distraction in the whirlwind of my emotions. I thought he was the love of my life. He took good care of me and made sure I went to school clean, uniform neatly pressed. He always made sure I had spending money and bus fare. So I did not need anything else in my life. And yet I felt so empty. So depressed. I cared less and less about things that mattered before, like schoolwork. It seemed like all I would do was go to school and sleep. Before I knew it, I was out of school with nothing to show for it. For the first time in my life, I began to believe with all my heart that I was a 'nobody'. And John began to treat me like I was a thing, a possession. I suppose he felt that giving me money meant that he had purchased me. We had a disagreement outside my home one day. He jump-kicked me in my chest and ran up the street in the village. I did not see him again until three days later. When he came to my house, my mother spoke to him and then urged me to go speak with him. I refused, reminding her that he kicked me in my chest. But she still felt I should give him another chance. John did not care for me. My speech – as affected as it was – began to deteriorate at an alarming rate. I was no longer able to read, spell or write well. I had resisted it all my life. Now the weight of *Dummy Diana* pressed hard upon my shoulders, breaking my bones and squashing me like dirt under the planter's boot.

Chapter 7
First Love's Bite

Ironically, it was dirt that began to liberate me. Specifically, the red, fertile soils of St. Lucy, the most northern parish of the island. Not too long after I finished school and had landed a job as a seamstress at Hooper's Garment Factory, I met a man by the name of Guy Nicholls. He was about six years my senior and he worked on plantation estate lands at Friendship as a head farmer contracted by the Barbados Agricultural Management Corporation. I met Guy playing dominoes in the village, at the house of a family friend. He took notice of me and invited me to join the game. I declined, but it sparked a conversation between us that seemed to be mutually pleasing. I remember him asking me why my face looked so serious most of the times. For some reason I felt I could trust him to share a little of my frustration. As the words eased from my mouth, it didn't take Guy long to pick up on my speech disability. And yet, I believed this drew him to me more.

I listened to him describe the fields where he worked. He was passionate about his job and as he spoke, colorful images of varying food crops, ripening fruit trees and fresh, clean air sprang up in my mind. He explained to me he needed additional help and invited me to come work with him. I considered the dead-end job I was working. I considered where I was in life and how far away my dreams seem to have drifted… like if the east coast waves had taken them straight back to the coast of West Africa. I was poor and could see no way out. So Guy's invitation moved my heart. I said to myself, "Yes, this is the one to help me out of my low life, or at least help me get out of this village!" We became good friends with no attachments at first.

It did not take long for me to get into the new job. I planted vegetables, helped Guy to plant the sugar canes and to reap them when they matured. Our friendship morphed into a romantic relationship and a year later, Guy decided to do the next "honorable" thing after marriage. He asked my parents for their consent to let me live with him on the estate. I expected my dad, who was a stubborn, no-nonsense person, to say many things to Guy that day. I did not expect one of those things to be "yes". My dad, who refused to let any man come around his house to speak to his daughters, was giving Guy consent to take me away from my home. I was too giddy-headed with happiness to give daddy's strange response much thought. Perhaps he saw in Guy someone who was hardworking, ambitious, and handled enough money that the entire family could benefit from some day.

Whatever the reason, my dad's reaction made it easy for me to give my life and my heart to Guy. I moved in with him and we lived as man and woman. For the first time, I was responsible for managing a household, a far cry from life in Belleplaine where I had no major domestic responsibilities. I now had to cook, clean house, wash clothes and take care of

Guy's personal needs. Guy would also call on me to assist him with managing the estate. I worked not just for him, but also with him, and the workers who would daily come to the estate respected me. Guy was intimate with the earth and with nature. It seemed that everything he touched with his hands produced a bountiful harvest. The pumpkins seemed larger. The tomatoes and cucumbers, the yams and sweet potatoes were plentiful. Even the animals prospered. I was happy being a part of this newfound freedom.

By the following year, 1983, I too began to blossom. I became pregnant with my first child. Guy was so happy and gave me everything I wanted. On April 18th, 1984, I gave birth to a beautiful baby girl, Victoria. She became my entire world; nothing could take her place. Naturally, being away from my village meant that first-time mothering was all the more difficult. I tried to keep up with the housework but was no longer able to work in the fields, and for this, Guy began to resent me. At first, it was the subtle cold shoulder. Eventually it grew to him verbally abusing me. He went as far as depriving me of food and clothing. I began to see that my real worth to him was as a field laborer and a warm body at night, not as his woman, not as the mother of his child. I later found out that his family resented me for coming in between him and them, where money was concerned. Before I came into the picture, Guy worked, but his father and brother controlled his money. Naturally, I influenced him to break away from this and stand on his own as the head of our household. They put pressure on him and in turn, he took it out on me. He would leave the house after work and not return until very late at night. I was left alone on an estate many times with a baby weeks old. It played with my mind. Darkness began to invade my thoughts.

One evening in particular, I waited up for Guy to return home. "I'm going to kill him! I'm going to kill him!" was all that was on my mind. I went to the kitchen, removed a carving knife from a drawer, and made my way to the bedroom. I had it in mind to stab him as soon as he touched me.

When Guy eventually came home, a strong stench of rum emanated from his pores, yet the stench could not mask an unfamiliar female perfume on his clothes. Seething with anger, my teeth clenched, I asked him where he had been. "Dat ain't none of your business; furthermore, I want yuh to leave my place. I ain't love you nomore!" he yelled.

My head overheated with anger and my heart overflowed with so much pain that I pushed him. He stumbled, regained control and pressed his weight upon me. I raised the knife towards Guy's throat and out of nowhere, it seemed, his brother appeared and took the knife from my hands. Guy and I started to fight. He pushed me so hard, that I struck my head on a board. I was not able to move anymore and he began to kick me all over my body, beat me all in my head and face. His brother did not pull him off me and I fainted. When I regained consciousness, it was morning.

In the weeks that followed, our relationship continued to nose-dive. As much as I was feisty and willing to give as many blows as I had to take, I was afraid of what could happen to Victoria in the midst of our confusion. I asked my mother if I could return home. She told me I had made up my bed with Guy, now I must lie in it. My father also refused my return, until he heard about the physical abuse I was suffering. He then permitted me to come home on one condition. I had to leave the baby behind for her father to take care of her.

The thought of death seemed like heaven compared to the hell I was experiencing on the farm. I remember sitting in the gallery of the house and crying for an entire week, my tears falling on Victoria as I rocked her back and forth. Guy turned off the stove, cut the electricity and denied me food. He denied me only because I could not be in the field anymore to help plant vegetables, cut canes or pick up the vegetables.

After that week, there were no more tears left to cry. I had died a million deaths and there was nothing in me left to give my baby. I could not take her with me, based on my father's instructions. I could not stay at the house, based on her father's instructions. I was a broken woman. A shell of my former self, physically and emotionally drained. So I had to do what I felt was the only thing left to do. When Victoria was a month old, I bathed her, dressed her and packed separate bags with our clothes. Guy was moving around the house that day, clueless to what was going on in my mind. By this time, it was clear that he was seeing someone else, though he only admitted to having a female friend. As soon as Guy was about to cross my path, I threw the baby into his unsuspecting arms. He caught her, his mouth open in shock.

By the time he realized what had happened, I was down the street in a stranger's car – someone with whom I had hitched a ride. I then caught a bus to Bellepaine, St. Andrew, back to my parents' house, where in solitude, I would wrestle with God to be merciful to me and let me live with my child again, or be merciful to me and let me die, so I could be spared this pain.

36　　Ain't No Dummy Around Here

Part Two
God in the Valley

38　Ain't No Dummy Around Here

Chapter 8
Gi' Me Back Me Chile

Throughout the West Indies, we black people have different ways of dealing with the dead. In islands such as Jamaica and St. Vincent, people do not mourn for the dead as we do in Barbados. They celebrate the life of the deceased in ways similar to our African ancestors, with dancing in the streets, with drums, with steel-pan and with revelry. The dead are now free from a life of hardship and suffering. There are no more tears to be shed, no more burdens to carry. Growing up in Barbados, funerals were a solemn occasion. The only music heard was the organ pipes of the Anglican Church, as we droned the hymns 'It is Well with My Soul' and 'Psalms 46'. Dressed in black and packed together like sardines in a can, we stood there in the church with our fans…

I saw myself being lowered in the grave, and the gravediggers began to shovel dirt on top of me. It was the dirt of every insult I received from Guy, of my father telling me to come home but leave my daughter behind. It was the dirt of a kick to the chest and other forms of physical abuse I received from men in my life. It was the dirt of Mrs. Drakes' family laughing at me, denying me food, depriving me of childhood fun and putting me to carry out urine pans every morning. It was the dirt of *Dummy Diana*. "Dummy yuh dummy, yuh can't talk, you will be nothing. You not smart enough yuh dummy! Get from in front of me until yuh learn to talk! Yuh dummy! Yuh dummy!"

I was suffocating. With my last gulp of air, I reached upward and pulled myself to a reality without my child in my arms. I got out of bed with only one thing on my mind. Go to St. Lucy and retrieve Victoria.

As I reached the farmhouse and shouted for Guy to come out, a familiar female face came to the door, dresses casually, as if she was living there. Here was the face of a woman Guy had nicknamed "Just-A-Friend". She approached me menacingly, like a guard dog protecting its master's house. "Why de hell you come back here for? Guy don't want you!" she yelled at me. "He tell me he don't love you, and you ain't getting back your baby. She is mine now. You throw she at Guy . She mine now".

I forgot I was a human that day and began to shout out for everyone to hear me. I cursed her and threatened to hurt her badly if she did not give me back my child. I knew I didn't have any place to take the baby, I had nowhere to go. But as the woman ran back inside of the house and picked up baby Victoria, every maternal bone in my body bid me to take back my child and run. The news of my presence spread like wild fire throughout the plantation grounds. Guy's voice was soon heard screaming, "Give Diana back she child." I did not realize it, but I had been marching from the house to the street and back, perspiration dripping from me, as if to wash away my fear and anxiety. I felt like I was in another world. It was as if I was dreaming. Only this was a nightmare, and I so badly wanted to wake up.

Guy took the child from Just-A-Friend and gave her to me, along with a bag containing a few of her belongings. I clung tightly to Victoria, walked up the street and sat down under a mango tree. I stared at the baby, who with all the commotion around her had begun to fret and cry. I too cried and became delirious when one by one, neighbors started congregating around me. All that was swarming my mind were the words, "If I die, you die, If I live you live. But nobody taking my child away from me today". One neighbor spoke up. "Diana, where you will take the child?" Another asked, "Diana you can't go back at your father?" Yet another begged me to give the child back to Guy. I wanted to scream.

As I was sitting, I saw Guy walking towards me. He came to me and said, "Give me the little girl." I angrily replied, "No, she is mine!" "She's mine too; look, I want you to come back with me and raise my baby," he told me, in a tone I had not heard for some time, a tone of familiarity, of affection even. Could I trust him? Or was he trying to trick me?

We sat there, under the trees in Friendship, St Lucy, for what seemed to be hours. As my anxiety began to dissipate, I wondered if I should cause my baby to suffer because I was suffering too. She did not ask to be brought into this world, this precious little thing curled up in my lap. I kissed her and told her she did not deserve to be hurt. I handed Victoria back to her father, got up from where I was sitting, and waited for a bus to take me back to Bellepaine.

Chapter 9
Double Delight

I remember brighter nights growing up in Bellepaine, St. Andrew. I remember stars like diamonds scattered across the black, velvet tapestry which hung over our heads. I remember how as children, we would spread out our crocus bags, lie down in the street and stare up at the great expanse to see a pitching star. It seemed like pitching stars were a lot more common, back then. Boys and girls alike would make wishes on these special stars. We girls would wish for the same things: marriage and children. I specifically had in my mind that I wanted all of my children to come from one man. Somehow, this was impressed upon my mind from as early as I could remember, though I had not rationalized why until later. Looking back, I saw the hurt that it caused my family. My mother was not allowed to raise all of her offspring under one roof because my father insisted he was not raising another man's child. Ironically, he did not father the children he produced outside of his marriage to my mother. This would cause conflict between us siblings. So wishing on that pitching star for this to never be my lot, for all my children to come from one man, was important to me and though trivial to some persons, was the main reason why I consented to go back to Guy. Yes, he mistreated me. Yes, he was abusive. Yes, I was quite sure he did not truly love me. But I went back to him because I was a mother now, and I had convinced myself that

Victoria tied me eternally to her father.

Not long after my return to the project in St. Lucy, we decided to move to another project, this time in St. Philip. Unlike the former one, this farm had cows and chickens, and the milk and eggs, which we produced, helped to fortify Victoria. She started to grow quickly. However, the isolated location of the farm meant that it could fall victim to praedial larceny. I convinced Guy that this was no place for me to be alone with a young baby. I was very much alone because he would leave me regularly to go out with friends. It angered me but I tried hard not to let my daughter see me fighting with her father. I believed God worked things out on my behalf because someone did eventually break into the farm and made off with some of the livestock. This scared Guy and he decided the farm was not safe. We moved.

We kept moving around from project to project in those early years, and each move seemed to land us somewhere better. Even though the relationship was not a happy one, Guy still seemed to appreciate the help I could offer him on the estates, and we never lacked food in those early years. I was also beginning to have confidence in myself again and would open up to people on the estates, talk with them, laugh with them.

From, St. Philip to St. Joseph to St. John and then St. George, we moved from government estates to private farms. Each time, I met more people and made friends with persons of varying ages and social backgrounds. My narrow perspective on life began to expand. My life as a woman began to open up as the knowledge I was gaining began to empower me. Guy noticed it too but he was far from pleased. He tried to control me by cursing me and threatening my life whenever he saw me talking to anyone, whether it was a man, woman or child.

The year 1987 was a unique year for us. I became pregnant with twins and had no idea about the twins part until I was eight months pregnant. I probably would not have known until later, had it not been for the fact that my doctor was concerned I was putting on too much weight and too quickly. Her concern was allayed when an x-ray confirmed the double blessing. I laughed when I remembered how as children, I would not eat anything resembling a twin. No twin bananas, no twin figs, no twin ackees. No not me! Anybody who ate any twin fruit would eventually get twin babies, we told ourselves in the village.

Nevertheless, I welcomed the news. I would have to start thinking differently in terms of family and household management. The Lord made this time of my life bright for me by allowing people to be generous. I received gifts in double portions and on October 7th 1988, I received in my arms, two healthy, identical baby girls, Christine and Crystal.

My joy of returning home with my babies was short-lived. God knows they meant the world to me. But Guy was sleeping around with other women again and his mess was landing on my doorstep.

One day, a woman came to the house. She wanted to put my fears at ease by telling me that she was just a friend (look at this, another Just-A-Friend!) and that I should ignore rumors. She even proceeded to ask me how the babies were doing. I stared at her.

"I know you, you came to the hospital with Guy to look for me, not so?" I asked her. "Yes, yes!" she responded, hopeful that this was a sign of no bad blood between us.

I stared at her again. "By the way, no one talked to me about you. I never heard of any rumors until you showed up at my place today. I am not vex with you, so please leave my house," I told her and shut the door. As soon as she left the house, I called Guy on his phone, told him what had just happened and stated to him very clearly that it was over between us. Guy returned home in 30 minutes and begged me not to leave him. I gave him a nasty look and demanded he tell me what he was prepared to do to stop me from leaving. I was expecting some half-baked plea about getting his act together and leaving out the outside women. I was not expecting him to say to me, "Let we get married, Diana, me and you, let we get married".

Chapter 10
Tied Up in a Knot

My father told me I would become just like my mother, plenty of children behind me. Imagine him saying that, being the one to father eight more of her children, after meeting her with three! So my three children, all born by the time I was 23, made him feel like his prediction would become truth. I shared that prediction with Guy on a few occasions and he decided to slap me in the face with it whenever it suited him. "I goin' breed yuh with nuff children and nobody will want you. You will be just like your mother," he would tell me in an attempt to maintain control over my life.

Here I was at the seamstress getting measured for my wedding dress. A few months had passed since Guy's sudden proposal of marriage. It was the second time I had come to fit my dress and she could not understand why I was gaining so much weight and so quickly. I knew, but I could not bear to say it aloud. She looked up at me with a smirk on her face. "Diana, you pregnant? That is why you getting so fat?" I tried to keep in the tears. "Yes," I told her, with my head hung low, ashamed. She pried some more and I told her I was afraid of people laughing at me and saying that I was a nobody. *Dummy Diana* gone and breed four times from a man that don't even treat she good.

Victoria was five years of age and the twin girls were six months. I was already three months pregnant and bursting.

My wedding day was one of the saddest days of my life… and I would have had a few by then. The event itself was massive, over 300 people, some invited, and many others who invited themselves. The most humiliating part of it was my family. They took over the show without any regard for my own feelings. Everyone ate, drank and enjoyed themselves, everyone except Guy and me. No one served us and all of the food, cakes and drinks ran out. Were pregnancy hormones making me feel so low? Why was this not the magical day about which every girl dreamed? I felt so trapped, like I was a rose crushed in the dust of the earth. The morning after, I was famished but we had nothing to eat. Guy and I had spent the night at a guesthouse in St. John. He joined a few friends to go down by the sea to pick seaweed from off the rocks. That is what I had to eat the day after the wedding. Seaweed.

The following weekend, a big party was kept at my parents' house for all those who did not attend my wedding. Guy and I were not invited.

Shelly-Ann, our fourth daughter, was born the year after, 1990. She made me feel so full with joy, despite everything else going on in my life. All my daughters cemented one thing in my life, that I was a mother and that all I had to go through was for them.

Chapter 11
Mr. Codrington

I soon got into a routine of raising four young children on a single income, Guy's. By then I had moved away from helping Guy in the farming business and devoted myself to being a full-time mother and homemaker. I had a kitchen garden and I would grow herbs and vegetables on a small scale to feed my family and make a little income on the side, usually keeping my sales within the community. We were renting a house in St. George by this time. Watching my children grow made me thirsty for something more for my family. I believed it was time for us to stop moving around. We needed to secure somewhere for ourselves and I needed Guy to understand that what he was bringing in was not cutting it.

One hot day, I looked through my kitchen window to see an old man farming the land. On his land stood a small, old house. I had been making some coconut punch and I decided to go over to him and inquire if he wanted a glass of punch. As I spoke with him, I picked up a warm and friendly personality. He smiled at my offer of refreshment and without hesitation he said, "Yes please, thank you." I asked him for his name and as I offered him the punch he said, "My name is Mr. Codrington". He drank all of the punch and complimented me on its taste. I thanked him.

The next day I saw Mr. Codrington again, working in his ground. "Diana, ain't no dummy around here! Open up your mouth and speak", I told myself. I worked up the confidence to go and speak with him and asked him if he was selling the house. He stood upright with a pensive look on his face and spoke in a very mannerly tone of voice. "I'm not sure, I would have to speak with my wife."

It was something. And something was better than nothing. As soon as Guy came home, I told him about the man and the house. Guy was all for it. It did not take Mr. Codrington long to get back to me with a decision. The very next day, he came to the house, stood at the door, looked me in my eyes and told me, "Yes, we will sell it to you and your family". He eventually settled at selling me the house for $5,000 Barbados dollars, and renting me the land. I could not keep back the tears. The small house was not in the greatest condition so we decided that we would eventually build over something affordable. I remember standing outside of our home with my daughters around me, looking up into the sky and saying to God, "Father, please hear me, if you can ever bring me out of this dust and help me to become who you want me to become… and give me a little house, not even a big one. I will serve you all the days of my life". That day, hope pierced my heart. Up until then it was as if only Diana the mother was alive, and barely trying to keep her head above water for the sake of her children. But the rest of me, up until that moment, was as good as dead. Was I saying to God I wouldn't serve Him if He did not come through with a house for us? Was I holding God to ransom? No, it was I who needed to be rescued.

I was so desperate for my family and myself. From that moment, I felt like better had to come, and better would come. God would make a way. I kept praying.

Guy decided to go for a loan from a commercial bank so that we could purchase the property from Mr. Codrington. I remembered I had a good friend, Winfield, who had promised me from the time we were in our teens, that he would one day become a good carpenter and would build himself a house and one for me too. I contacted him to remind him of that promise. He chuckled and replied, "Yes, Diana, I promised you I would and I don't intend to break that promise". He also agreed to build it free of charge and only requested that I give him a meal while he was on the job.

Not long after, Winfield gave me a list of materials to rebuild the house. He said to me that he would begin work as soon as he received the materials. Guy worked on getting what we needed and that very week a truck pulled up to our new property to offload the building materials. My faith was energized by how quickly things were falling into place for us.

In six months' time, what was a tiny old house was now a beautiful, wooden three-bedroom house. As I watched the work being done and the materialization of what was to be our first family home, I could not help but see myself in a similar process. I was that old broken-down house. I felt aged and broken in my marriage. I felt the physical and emotional strain of having to wonder every single day how I was going to feed my children. Looking back, I fought hard to remember a time where my happiness was greater than my hurt, where my passion was not stifled by pain. Could God really have a plan for my life? Yes, I was that old broken down house, in such a bad state that no patchwork would be enough to bring me back to glory. I needed to be completely made over. I needed a skilled carpenter to fashion a Diana that was somebody special, someone worthy of love and respect. I did not know that all along my journey, God was still loving me. That day in 1991, when I saw what man could do with a hammer and a chisel, I asked God to come into my heart and remake me into the person He wanted me to be. I surrendered all.

Chapter 12
Baby Steps

My "yes" to God did not translate immediately into a "yes" to church. Looking back, one of the things that deterred me was that in my small community almost everyone went to church. Yet quite a few of them were nasty, spiteful gossipers and carnal in so many other ways. Of course, I used this as an excuse to stay away from 'a church full of hypocrites' as I would call them. But more than that, the pressures of home crowded my mind. Financially we were still struggling. Guy used to bring home $100 a week. Imagine trying to stretch $100 to feed a family of six and still clothe them and take care of other household needs. Guy became more and more like a ticking time bomb, exploding without warning.

I starting to send the little ones to Sunday school. They enjoyed it very much and would continually bug me to come with them. One day, in 1992, I decided to stop making excuses and join my daughters. It was Saturday and my children were taking part in a Sunday school program the following day. I was over at a family member's house, helping to do chores. I was moving a cabinet when suddenly, a pane of glass shifted from the cabinet, fell forward and was about to land on top of Victoria. Instinctively I put out my hands to shield my child and the glass broke, cutting me deeply on one hand.

I was rushed to seek medical attention and ended up getting several stitches. During that entire episode, all I could think of was how I had just made a decision to go to church with my children and now it seemed like the devil was trying his best to keep me away. It made me more determined to go, and on Sundays, I made it my business to sit next to my children in the pews of the community church.

Never one to be idle, I soon volunteered to clean the church. This was the start of my service in God's house. The more I cleaned the church, the more God was cleaning me up. I felt like cleaning was really the only thing I could do to serve God. My self-esteem was low and I believed I could not be called on to pray nor read a Bible lesson aloud. But I was very good at cleaning the church. One day, the pastor approached me and asked me if I would be the church secretary. I laughed. "Pastor, I can't read or write." "You can do all things through Christ who gives you strength," the pastor replied, but he did not pursue the issue at that time.

Sometime passed before he called on me again, this time to read a Bible lesson during a church service. I declined but he persisted and, not wanted to be the center of attention for too long, I gave in. As I began to read the lesson, the congregation began to laugh at me so badly. I was so ashamed of myself that I began to cry. The pastor ordered the congregation to apologize for being so insensitive but my heart was already cut in half. As soon as I returned home, I went on my knees and said to God "Never again You make me shame, I will never read or do anything in Your church, I'm a dummy."

I did not want to trust anyone in the church again after that fiasco, but the pastor did not give up hope that God would do a miracle in my life and so he continued to give me small assignments to do things in the house of the Lord.

Chapter 13
Encounters with the Holy Spirit

Oh, how I loved soap operas like 'The Bold and the Beautiful' and 'Generations'! I watched them religiously every day. I was so hooked on soaking in the drama on the screen – family squabbles, love, sex, betrayal, friendships - that even when the church was in a period of fasting, I would incorporate my television time into the fasting schedule.

One afternoon, during such a time, a friend stopped by and suggested we watch some movies. Normally I would have said 'yes' but this time around I declined and told him it was because I was fasting.

My friend looked at me and said, "Fasting what! How you can be fasting and watching you soap-operas?" I was livid. The audacity of this unbeliever to tell me what I should or should not be doing as a Christian! I thought to myself that God could never use my friend to speak to me; so I ordered him to leave my house. The anger melted into serious conviction as I sat and reflected on what my friend said and on my awful reaction. I turned the television off and began to pray, sincerely asking God to clean me and make me into who He wanted me to become.

While praying, I began to have an assurance of God's presence with me and in my spirit, I heard these words, "I am going to stir up people to do mighty things in the kingdom. When God gives it, no man can take it."

As I was praying and hearing the word of God, I asked Him why he was choosing me. "Are there no other Christians in the Church you can use?" I pleaded with Him. I opened my eyes and suddenly, a bright little light appeared in the distance. The light approached me and in front of it were three ugly creatures; each had two big eyes and long, dangerous-looking teeth. They flew toward my head. I shouted out, "Jesus, Jesus, the blood of Jesus save me!" This made the demons behave more violently; they hovered over me trying to eat my head. I continued to shout out, "Jesus, save me, the blood of Jesus". The light I had first seen became brighter. It too approached me and overshadowed the three killers from darkness. I did not know what the light was, but its presence seemed to consume everything in its way. It scattered the demons, then rested on me.

Immediately, I jumped to my feet and skipped all through the house, praising God and thanking Him for His deliverance. I felt empowered. The Spirit of the Lord was upon me and had anointed me. He led me to a portion of Scripture that remains with me to this day.

> *"Let not your heart be troubled; you believe in God, believe also in Me. In My Father's house are many mansions; if it were not so, I*

> would have told you. I go to prepare a place for you. And if I go and prepare a place for you, I will come again and receive you to Myself; that where I am, there you may be also. And where I go you know, and the way you know." Thomas said to Him, "Lord, we do not know where You are going, and how can we know the way?" Jesus said to him, "I am the way, the truth, and the life. No one comes to the Father except through Me."
>
> **John 14:1-6**

My life was never the same again. I opened my heart and allowed Jesus to have greater reign in my life.

One day the Lord used me to go down into the village to prophesy to a lady in her 60's. I was to tell her that she was going to die. The Lord had told me He would send me out to speak on His behalf but I fought with Him and said, "No! Lord I can't go, no way, nobody would listen to me. More people are in the church, why You want to use me to give that sad news?" I fought and fought until I felt someone hold me by my hand. That "someone" pulled me until I got to the lady's house.

The lady was my best friend's mother. As soon as I reached in front of the lady's house, I greeted her. She replied, "Good morning Diana, I was here waiting on you, I was just in the garden fixing up until you come." My eyes opened wide with shock.

"Come on in my daughter!" she exclaimed. "Tell me what the Lord told you to say to me." I was afraid because she was living near a shop where men would be drinking alcohol. The lady took me into her house, straight to her bedroom and said, "Tell me what God told you about me".

I shut my eyes tightly and said, "The Lord told me to let you know that He loves you. You went through a lot in your life and He is ready to take you with Him. He said you will be sick and you'll go to the hospital and He will take you home with Him, without pain. He also said that your soul is ready and He cannot allow you to remain on the earth and lose your salvation. He said you have given Him your life in your older years and He has received it. So prepare yourself for His calling!"

I could see that she was at peace with the message I delivered. We sat there in her bedroom and prayed. As I was leaving her house, my body began to shake. From that day, I was never the same again. The Holy Spirit began to be with me in a very strong way, wherever I went.

About two weeks after I prophesied to the lady. She took ill and her family took her to the hospital. She remained in the hospital for about two weeks. Two weeks before she died, she called all of her children and grandchildren, telling them to share and do not fight for anything, to be good to each other.

I clearly remember that same day. Her son, who was my friend, came and said to me, "I thought you said that my mother was going to die? Well, I want you to know, she said she's going home so we are not to fight but be good to each other".

I said to him, "I'm sorry, but it wasn't me that told your mother she was going to die; it was God!" That same very night, the doctor called the family and asked them to come and see their mother. It was reported that she had gone to the bathroom, returned to her bed to lie down and without a word, had slipped away to meet her heavenly Savior.

The family began running to me to tell me that the prophetic word I shared had come to pass. I said again that it was not me but God who had that message for their mother. I was scared but God continued to use me to share His Word with others and I saw many miracles taking place around me. How awesome is our Lord!

Chapter 14
Health Scares

Of faith and flight. That is how I could best describe the next decade and beginning years of my Christian walk. Barbadian households were taken through a different kind of processing in the early 1990s, when an economic recession forced the then Government to agree to a debt restructuring exercise under the watchful eyes of the International Monetary Fund. Among other things, civil servants were forced to take an eight per cent cut to their salaries. Some persons lost their jobs. Families were under real pressure.

Things were tremendously hard for my family. A considerable amount of Guy's income went to his parents and I had no help from my own relatives. My livestock had dwindled down to two pigs. My children were growing and had needs just like everyone else's children. I found myself doing a lot more praying in those years, crying out to God to help me take care of my family.

Another area I suffered in was my health. What was strange about it was that I could not put a name to anything I was going through. There were days I would be sitting at the table and my children would be talking to me. I would be good one moment, and the next, I would pass out on the floor. The first 'black out' occurred soon after I gave birth to the twins but they increased in frequency when I had all of my children.

One day, as I was cleaning the church, my head began to hurt so badly, I thought I was going to die. I felt something rummaging through my head. I held onto my head and I felt it moving. It ran around my head, down my face, into my jaw, back up and then down my nose. As I felt it in my nose, I began to blow and it came through one of my nostrils. When I looked at it, it was a clot of blood which was black and blue.

I went to the doctor the following day to find out what caused that to happen and the doctor sent me for an x-ray to see if I had experienced some sort of trauma. The doctor told me that if the clot of blood did not find its way out, I would have been a dead woman.

The health scare that frightened me the most was when I lost my voice completely. I remember one evening my voice started to go and then it was gone. Completely gone. I tried and tried but nothing would come out. The thought came to go take a bath. Maybe stress was the cause behind what was happening. I tried to be brave and to rationalize what was happening to me. Deep down inside however, I was so scared. Was my childhood disability finally taking a turn for the worse? Was the loss of my voice permanent? If it did come back, would I revert to the little broken girl from Bellepaine, St. Andrew whose mother would push her away and tell her go learn to talk? Or whose neighbors would laugh at her calling her Dummy Diana? Fear gripped my heart as these thoughts assaulted my mind. For a few dark minutes I felt like an insecure girl trapped in an adult body. "Turn on the tap, Diana!" I was quickly jolted back to reality… and to remembering how that little girl would find comfort in God's arm. I cried out to Him. Silently I prayed for God to restore my voice. "Lord, if You give me back my voice I promise You I will do anything You want me to do. I will use my voice for You, God. Please Heavenly Father, You have been with me all these years, please hear my cry." My tears mixed with the water coming down on my skin. I began to tell God how much I loved Him. I began to sing without a voice and somehow, I became convinced that my voice would return. Fear was gone. I had faith! After I finished bathing, I turned off the pipe and the water stopped running. My voice came back, I called the names of my family, "Guy, Christine, Crystal…" The voice was getting louder and clearer, "Victoria, Shelly". This was a new voice God had given me and I promised him I would use it to honor Him.

Chapter 15
Two Pigs and a Visa

In the year 1993, I dreamt that I was flying on an airplane to the United States of America. I knew that although I did not have a travel visa, God was big enough to set things in motion for this dream to come true. Well, shortly after that dream, I suffered from a headache which lasted for 14 days. The pain was so bad I sought medical treatment from several doctors. All they gave me were tablets. I took so many tablets that I could no longer tell which made me feel worse, too many tablets or the headache. I would run and hide or push my head inside of barrels or go under the bed. Nobody could touch me; it was too overbearing. At one point I thought I would die.

A United Holiness Church had a special service and a prophet was ministering to the people. During his ministry, he called for people that suffered from backaches, stomach aches and headaches to make their way up to the altar to receive prayer for divine healing. So many people moved from their seats that I convinced myself the prophet could not have been talking to me. As soon as he was finished praying for the people, he shouted out, "There is someone else in here! The Lord says come and get prayed for, your headaches stayed on you for two weeks and would not leave".

I refused to move but then both he and the pastor of the church looked at me and ordered me to stand up. I did. As soon as I got up the prophet shouted, "The spirit is gone!" I sat back down and stared at him, wondering to what kind of spirit the man could be referring. Still in my thoughts, the prophet looked at me and ordered me to get up and come to him. "The spirit has come back" he added. I obeyed, even though I was somewhat skeptical. The minister began to prophesy to me, "The Lord showed me you are suffering from a headache that lasted for two weeks and sometimes you feel you are not normal. I looked at him and he said, "I see you with four children, you have four girls." I opened my eyes and questioned myself, "Did someone tell this man about me just now?" He continued to say, "I see you flying to America and … I see you driving, driving a white car." I knew I did not have a white car, so he could not mean me. He also said that my headache was going to leave me in seven days.

I did not respond but went to take my seat. After church was finished, I asked the pastor if he told the prophet about me and he said 'no'. One month later, I decided to step out in faith once more. I would go to the American Embassy to apply for a travel visa. It was really a step of faith but I held on to the dream and the word the prophet gave me. I had no money, no job, nothing to show how I would have been able to get this visa or sustain myself financially while abroad. I kept pigs but I only had two at that time.

My faith was encouraged when I wrote to my brother asking him to send me a letter of visitation. He did and I was able to then schedule an appointment at the embassy, where they would interview me and review my application form before granting or denying me entry into the USA. On the other hand, my family back home tried everything to discourage me. My mother had applied for a visa on several occasions before and was denied each time. An older sister too had applied but was not granted a visa. Imagine my presumption that things could work out in my favor. This is what they thought and told me. But it was not mere presumption, it was me acting on a word from God. I did not accept any negative reports, I held on to the Bible verse in Hebrews 11:1.

> *"Now faith is the substance of things hoped for, the evidence of things not seen."*

The morning of my appointment, I did not let anyone distract me. I got dressed and took my husband and last daughter with me. She was only three years old. I went in the office and filled out an application form presented to me. I told the truth on the form, no job… no bank account… no money. My named was called. I proceeded to one of the counters. The white gentleman behind the counter looked at me and asked, "Is that your husband, Ma'am?" glancing in the direction of Guy. I replied, "Yes." "Is that your daughter?" he continued to ask me. I said, "Yes." He then asked what else I had to show him. I presented to him the letter of invitation from my brother and told him my husband was the one who would sponsor my ticket and spending money. The officer questioned me about my job status. As he studied my face, I told him as confidently as I could that I had just built a house and that I kept pigs to help sustain my family.

He asked, "Pigs? How many pigs do you have?" I stuttered "Two pigs" and the officer took my stutter to mean something different. He shouted, "Ah, twenty-two pigs!"

I shook my head, but not another word would come out before he asked me the selling price for a pig. I answered that the going rate was $60.00 Barbadian dollars. The Embassy officer looked at me, smiled, told me "Good, that means you'll have some money to spend when you return," stamped my passport with an indefinite visa and told me "have a nice day". I left the embassy that day feeling like I was walking out of a dream. Like if something just happened to me that I had no part of, no control over. All I could sing in my heart was that my God was able and abundantly able.

The events of that day made for good conversation. My siblings were in disbelief. They could not figure out how they, with their jobs and savings, could be turned down and I, with nothing but two pigs, could get through. As I travelled and as time passed, I took my mother to get her visa and she was granted one. My husband, my children and eventually my grandchildren, all of them would receive their travel visas for the USA. Years later, I would grasp that God's act of opening America to me was all part of his plan for my life's purpose.

Chapter 16
Cut Down

God continued to show me things and events before they happened. It was happening to me on such a frequent basis that it was beginning to feel more to me like a burden rather than a blessing. So I wrestled with God. I did not feel in any way righteous. I was going to church but so many people, including myself, made me feel as if I did not belong in the church, as if I was not holy enough for God to use. I would beg God to take away this gift from me. I would beg Him to find someone else to use. I would tell Him that the church was filled with a whole set of righteous, refined women of God who He could use. I asked Him what He would want with a fighting, cuss-bird, dummy woman like me, a broken woman in a broken marriage with four children, poor and struggling. The only thing I could be good for was cleaning the church. And this I did contentedly.

One day, I was cleaning the church in preparation for an upcoming church service. A woman from the community that owned the land upon which the church was built, passed by and began to talk down to me. At the time I did not know the connection between her and the land. She was a vindictive, malicious woman and she was looking to pick a fight with me. "I don't care how much you clean that church, you all will still have to move from off my spot," she seethed at me.

I looked at her, stared her in the face and told her, "The Church that God built, the gates of hell shall not prevail against it." What I also did not know was that this same woman was related to Mr. Codrington, the owner of the land upon which my own house was built.

Confusion started to raise its ugly head in my quiet rural neighborhood. Word came to me that some of the neighbors resented my family and me because we were able to travel, a luxury for many poor families at the time. They started to say I was acting too big. One day, the same woman with whom I exchanged words at the church, passed by my house while I was sitting outside. She said, "Just how you come and find we, you got to go along and leave we. That same house you build, you will have to move it from off the land and go back which part you come from." I was so shocked. I never did this lady anything. I don't know what made me say it, but I took one look at the woman and told her, "You better leave me alone… someone is going to kill you. Someone is going to cut your throat." The woman scowled her face and lifted up her skirt at me in a vulgar manner. "You go along from here, you better repent, woman!" I shouted.

Guy and I used to keep dogs. Not long after my confrontation with the woman, I awoke one morning to find all seven of my puppies lying dead in the road, just outside of my house. I dressed myself and went straight to the church to tell the pastor what had happened. Again, I don't know what made me say it at the time but I told the pastor that God was going to punish the persons that killed my dogs. They would die or if they lived, their lives would not prosper. One night at a prayer service in the church, I stood up praying along with other members of the church. I was standing next to a particular member who I would later find out was involved in killing my dogs. As I was praying, I went into a vision and the Lord showed me the woman standing next to me, helping someone else to kill my dogs. When I came out of the vision, I confronted her but she denied it. "I had nothing to do with it, it was the lady that cursed you the other day. She gave them bread with rat poison and killed them," she frantically told me.

All I could do was leave these women in God's hands.

I confronted Mrs. Codrington weeks after about the rumors spreading in the community that I would have to move my house from the spot of land her husband had agreed to rent me to build my house. She too denied spreading any such rumors and told me that there was no truth to what I was suggesting. However, in my spirit, I knew she was lying. I went home and told my family that Mr. Codrington was going to be very sick and would die. I also told them that his wife was going to endure hardship because she agreed to let us build on their land, invest time and money that we could not afford without the help of a bank loan. Now she was walking about telling people we had to get off her property.

Two months later, the wicked woman who had killed my dogs and pestered me about having to "go back where I come from", got into a conflict with a man in the neighborhood.

Apparently, I was not the only one who found her to be an annoyance. The following week, she accompanied a friend of hers to the bus stop to catch a bus. On her way back home, while she was passing a cane field, a man struck her in the head with an object. As she was trying to run away from him, he knocked her down and she ended up in a gutter. The man left her there.

Soon after, a few men who were on a tractor saw her and drove into the neighborhood shouting for us to come quickly. We did not know if she was alive or dead at the time but several of us ran to the place they said she lay. When we got to the location, to our surprise, the woman could not be found. People became frightened. A boldness came over me and I told the group that we should go deeper into the cane field. They agreed and some men led the way. We pushed back the canes. Stalk after stalk, row after row we went, until we saw the woman lying flat on the ground. Her head was partially detached from her body and her throat cut right out. I remember the heat of the midday. I remember her children were part of the search group. They broke down in grief when they saw their mother. Her son ran out of the cane field and up the road, crying hysterically all the way.

My pastor was there standing, not too far from me. I went over to him and whispered to him that I knew what had happened. The pastor was aware of my revelatory gifts. He told me to say what I knew and I said, "While she was walking a man struck her from behind. As she was trying to run away he knocked her over into the gutter.

As the men on the tractor approached, this man ran and hid. While the neighbors on the tractor returned to the village for help, the man who attacked her took her up, brought her deeper into the cane field, put her to lie down on her face and chopped her neck off with a cutlass. She did not have chance to struggle."

On my way going home, my head began to hurt me and as soon as I reached my house, I saw a neighbor, a man bending over and cutting grass with a cutlass in his hand. I shouted to my pastor, "Pastor! It is him, he killed her!" but the pastor did not believe me. That very night, officers from the Royal Barbados Police Force stationed themselves in front of my patio, watching the man's house. By the morning, they arrested him and charged him for murder.

That very year, Mr. Codrington took ill to the point that he turned over his affairs to his wife. Mrs. Codrington, who had said there was no truth to the rumors about her wanting to get us off her land, served us notice to do just that. I did not fight it but committed the matter to God in prayer. I was very sad though, all that money that went towards building our home, now gone. We would lose what went into the foundation, the bathroom and the well. At least we could pick down the wooden structure and take it with us. But where would we find land that we could afford on a small single income?

Chapter 17
A Lump and a Leg

Our pastor went all out to assist Guy and me in searching for a new location to live. Eventually, our search took us to Jackson, St. Michael. A landlord for the area told us he had a house spot we could rent but it was at the back of some houses. We were somewhat put off by that but something was better than nothing. We decided to go look. How bad could it be? The following day, my husband and I went to meet the landlord to see the land. The spot was a mixture of a forest and a garbage dump. It was right on the edge of a gully filled with bush and there on the land were old cars, old vans, boulders, discarded wood and iron, even garbage. I was distraught. "No, I can't live here, I can't bring my children down here to live in this dump!" I cried to Guy and my pastor. My pastor pleaded with me, "Diana, I will help you fix it, clean it up, push away the old vehicles, build up the land and dig the foundation. With much trepidation, I gave in. Guy and I told the landlord we would take the land to put our home. Little did I know that that move would push me into a higher calling in God.

In 1995, Christine, one of the twin girls, came to me and said she felt a lump in her breast. She was still a little girl so I believed that I was the one who was scared, not her. I felt the area and the lump was the size of an ackee seed. I took her to a family doctor located in St. George, not far from where we used to live. The doctor gave me a form that would allow me to take Christine to the hospital to receive an operation for the lump to be removed. I took the paper and went home. Silently, I prayed to my Heavenly Father, not wanting to raise alarm among the children. I had faith that nothing was impossible for God to do as long as I believed.

While I was cooking that same afternoon, I heard a voice speaking to me which said, "My child." I answered, "Yes, please." The voice continued, "This is your Daddy, ask and it shall be given unto you. My hand is not too short, My ears are not too heavy that I can't hear." I began to weep and said, "God, I believe You can heal Christine the same way You healed Shelly when the girls were playing and the ball hit the glass and the glass fell on Shelly's hand as she was going for the ball. The glass cut her hand, near to a vein… and Daddy, You allowed me to place my hand on my child and pray and the blood stopped instantly and when I went to the doctor, he asked, 'How the blood stopped when a vein has been cut?' and I said to him, 'My Father in heaven healed her'. Shelly received stitches and I want to know if You can do the same healing for Christine."

My anxiety unraveled before the Lord and I opened up my heart to Him completely. As I was talking to him, I heard Him command me, "Turn off the stove and go lie down in Christine's bed until I tell you to move. When I tell you to move, bring her, take off her clothes and make her lie flat on her face in the same place you lay until I tell you when to tell her to move." I obeyed God fully. After I lay down for about thirty minutes. I heard God's voice say to me to bring Christine. I brought Christine in the house, she was outside playing. She was seven years old at the time.

I took off Christine's clothes, placed her in the same spot where I lay. I ordered her not to move until I told her to do so. After one hour, I went and found Christine sleeping in the same position I placed her. I woke her up, placed her to sit on the floor, put some olive oil set aside for prayer in my hands and began to anoint her breast. As I was anointing her breast, I felt the lump. I called the rest of the family into the room, Guy and the girls, and asked them to place their hands on the area where the lump was found.

I began to pray from the bottom of my heart. "Lord, you told me all I have to do is ask of You, well Lord, I am asking for You to heal my daughter as You are a God who heals. Nothing is too hard for You to do."

As I was praying, I felt the lump become smaller and smaller and as I moved my hands around her breast, the lump disappeared. No more lump! I placed Guy's hands and her sisters' hands to feel for the lump. They could feel nothing. No doctor, no hospital for Christine. It was the Lord that healed Christine that day, all by Himself. That miracle stood as testimony to my household that God was able to do all things. We could trust God for the impossible.

Our belief in God of the Impossible was tested in a major way later that same year. This time we needed a huge miracle for Guy.

I was in church a Sunday night praising God and suddenly I fell on the ground and straight into what seemed like a horrible nightmare. I was rolling around on the ground and before me, a big, black hole about six feet deep opened up. I rolled right to the edge of the hole and was about to fall in. I screamed, trying to hold on to anything my hands could reach, shouting, "Please, don't let me fall into that hole, it is deep and black!" The pastor, his wife and members tried to wake me out of the vision. They took me up from the ground and my head began to hurt so badly again. My pastor lifted me up in his arms, took me to his van and carried me home. I remember they wrapped my head with a piece of cloth and poured some Alcolado, a cooling liquid, on my head, before placing me in my bed. As they left, I said, "Goodnight." I remember seeing my husband and children standing over me and watching me. They were asking, "Mummy are you okay?" I said, "No, no, not good at all!" Another strange feeling came over me, I felt like I was not myself. With a voice of authority that did not sound like my own, I turned towards Guy and cried, "You stiffen your neck and harden your heart but it is hard for thee to kick against the pricks." I reached into the wardrobe and took out a green suit, one Guy could wear to church, or be buried in. "The Lord said there is going to be an accident but He is going to save you if you repent and turn from your wicked ways." After I said that, I fell back on the bed and in no time was fast asleep.

When I awoke from my sleep, it was about two hours later. My children told me everything I did. Guy had been so afraid he repented and asked God to save him at that time.

Two weeks after the prophecy about the accident, Guy and I had a brief conversation about a dream I had where I was driving his white car. He then went off to work. At the time he used to work for C. O. Williams Company driving a truck, delivering bricks to homes and businesses.

I remember going across to the neighbor's house to ask him about a driving matter as I was driving Guy's white car up and down the gap, trying to teach myself how to maneuver it. While in conversation with my neighbor, I heard sirens from an ambulance and fire engine. The emergency vehicles were speeding east, in the direction of the parish of St. Joseph. A pain gripped my stomach, my chest and my head. It cut off my breath. I started to shout out to God, "Please save Guy!" I had no idea why I said what I did, I heard nothing saying that it was Guy, but I continued to feel pain. I turned my attention to something else, trying to put the fear of something bad happening out of my mind. About 15 minutes later, I heard a truck driving into the neighborhood, it sounded like Guy's own, so I said in my mind that the accident could not have been Guy. Before that thought could allay the fear I was feeling, the truck came into my view and I saw it was not Guy's truck. Two men sprang out of their seats with the truck engine still running. They ran toward me. My knees began to buckle. Holding my stomach, I cried out, "Oh God, he dead, he dead?"

"We not sure", the men replied, "but we hear he feet break and probably he neck break." By then I was hysterical, I felt like I was on fire and I shouted, "Oh God, please save Guy, please save him!" My neighbors ran out to my assistance. My pastor, who had tried to reach me before the men, also came to console me. "Diana, do not lose hope, do not let go of your faith, Guy is not dead but his truck collided with a car being driven by a woman. She had a child with her," the pastor told me. He went on to say that in order to minimize the impact on the car – a greater collision would have sent the car over a bridge in the area - Guy swerved into an oncoming bus that was coming from St. Andrew. My pastor, who had visited the scene briefly before coming to me, said that the impact between the truck and bus caused the truck's steering wheel to be dislodged. He said that Guy, who was still breathing and able to talk, told him that he heard a voice telling him to shift, seconds before colliding into the bus. He did this and the steering wheel was forced into the back of his seat, missing his body entirely. The engine however became dismantled from its original place. It fell on Guy's feet, pinning him in the truck. Firemen had to remove him from the carnage with the Jaws of Life.

A fresh fear of God fell on me as I reflected on the prophetic word I had given to Guy. I could not stop crying. On my way to the Queen Elizabeth Hospital I was still crying as I thought about this Great God whose words, which was so powerful, came to pass. When I reached the hospital, I saw Guy on a bed in the Accident and Emergency ward. Surprisingly, he was there smiling. I went over to him and all he was saying was,

"Thank Jesus, He saved me; I did not kill the woman and her child. Diana, you and the children came right in front of me, so I said 'No way!' I will die first before I take this woman and her child's life. That was the only choice I had." I looked down to his feet which were covered. When I removed the sheet of cloth, I saw one foot in a plastic covering. All the skin on his leg was rolled backward, exposing his flesh. His knee was dislodged from the socket. All I could do was look at Guy and hope in my heart that now he would give his heart to God. Only God could have pulled him through this ordeal. Medical staff came to take Guy into the operation theatre. So, I left and returned home to take care of the girls.

By the time I reached the house, my brain was fried, my emotions were all frayed and the sight of my girls broke my heart. I forgot in that moment that God was at work. I felt alone with these girls and cried out to God because I felt like He had forgotten me. Dark thoughts flooded my mind. My husband would not be able to work now. We were poor before the accident, now we would become destitute. I would not be able to take care of my babies. The care of these children would fall entirely to me, a woman who had nothing. My faith began to leave me. I started to shout to God, "Why, why now? I don't have anyone to feed my children, Why You allowed it to happen? You tell me You love me. Yes, You told me this accident would happen but I did not know it would be this bad!" I yelled, not caring who heard me. "I'm not working and my children can't eat!"

As I was crying and quarrelling with God, I heard a loud crashing noise in the house and my four frightened children ran toward me, right between my legs. I pulled them behind me. "Oh God, now they know that no man is in the house and they coming to kill us all now!" I was delirious, not thinking straight, sobbing, tears mixing with mucus running from my nose and down my face.

Slowly, I walked out of the living room and into the dining room. I looked in the corner of the house to see what had likely caused the loud noise. A plant that hung from the roof in a rope basket had dropped on its face and broken up. I took up the plant and stared at the basket, saying in my heart that this could never have happened because too many roots were wrapped around the rope basket and roots were also spread across the ceiling of the house. How could this be? No way a plant could lose itself from a basket that was full of roots to fall on the ground. I tried to push the plant and lift up the vine again but it would not budge.

My oldest daughter Victoria said to me, "Mummy, God is vexed, you don't trust Him and He told you about this in a vision before it happened; Mummy, God will take care of us, just believe it."

I held my daughters close to me and said, "I love you all." Victoria was eleven years old, the twins Christine and Crystal were seven years old and Shelly-Ann was six years old. Still, all I could think about that night, was how much harder my life would be because I did not have a job.

Chapter 18
Divine Healing

Divine Healing
Trust and obey, Trust and obey
for there is no other way
than to trust and obey.

I heard that song for the first time as a child attending a revival in my village. I held on to its message, that Jesus wanted me to trust Him in trying times and obey Him, knowing that His plans for me were special, were in my best interest. Over 20 years later, I still found it difficult to put my complete trust in a God I could not see or touch. How patient He was with me, seeing me through every fearful time of my life: the fear of losing my first child; the fear of someone harming my children; the fear of dying in a loveless marriage; the fear of having nowhere to live; the fear of saying "yes" to God and to service in his Church; of trial after trial, of sickness, of brokenness, of threats from others, of false accusations, of Guy getting into a serious accident that would cause him to lose his job, leaving our family without any income. These trials in life tested my faith in God's ability to keep me and all that concerned me.

The day after Guy's major truck accident which badly damaged his foot and leg, I received a call from a friend telling me that he had recommended me for a job at the Royal Pavilion Hotel as a domestic worker. The timing of

God could not have been better. I thankfully accepted the job. Guy's severe injuries resulted in him staying in the hospital for three months. Up until that point, I did everything for my children. I was there when they awoke, I saw them off to school and I was there to see them to bed. Now, with Guy away and with the offer of this job, I had to ask the neighbor to keep my children until I returned home. That was not easy for me, having to beg people to take them to school. Sometimes, I worked nights and had to walk a dark, lonesome road to get to my home, since no public transportation came that far into the village.

When Guy eventually came home on crutches, the Lord gave me a daily assignment to lay my hands on Guy's feet until He told me to take them off. I was to do so every morning and evening. Every time I placed my hands on Guy's feet, my entire body would tremble. It felt to me as if all of Guy's pains would come into my hands and stomach. When the pain became too much for me to bear, I would cry out to God, then I would feel this immense nudge from the Holy Spirit to remove my hands. I did this each day for about nine months, believing that as I obeyed God, He would show up for Guy in a way that only He could do. During those long months, Guy would often look up to me with discouraged eyes and say, "Diana, I will never walk again," and each time I would look at him and reply, "That's not what God said, He said 'You will walk again and be stronger.'" Guy's pains which God was allowing me to identify with, were more acute than the pain I experienced giving birth to my children.

Then one day in 1996, the breakthrough came in yet another unexpected fashion. That morning I left Guy home lying down in the chair. I knew he could not walk without help, not even to take himself to the bathroom. So I would put the necessary things within reach to facilitate his basic needs.

The evening, I returned from work, physically tired but psyching up myself mentally to take care of Guy and the children's needs. Heading straight to the kitchen to prepare the evening's family meal, I called out for Guy. After a few minutes, I realized I was hearing no response from him. I began to think the worse things when I searched each of the bedrooms and could not find him. I went to the back of the house, shouting, but there was no response. As I approached the back yard, I saw fresh dirt in a heap, as if someone had been digging. I shouted, "Guy you in there?" I went closer to the pile of dirt and saw there was a hole. When I peered into the hole, there was Guy. He had been digging a well. When I questioned him on what he was doing, Guy said he heard a voice telling him to get up from his bed, go to the backyard, retrieve a hoe and fork and start digging. To this day I can't figure out how Guy managed to dig a six feet deep hole in our yard, while still using his crutches. But he obeyed that voice.

After the accident, Guy did not return to delivery work or driving trucks. Instead he switched to masonry. He began to walk and as he walked, he began to continue building and expanding our family home, changing it from a timber house to a wall house. In the process, he became an A-class mason.

He never took classes. Right there on the house spot, the Holy Spirit taught him how to work as a mason and this new skill opened tremendous financial doors for the family.

Part Three
Accepting the Call

Chapter 19
Jackson Nazarene

The miracles I saw God perform in my family as the years passed not only built my faith, but my confidence to share about my faith. When I first entered the church, I felt so small and insignificant, but I learned that I was precious in God's eyes. If that was not so, why would He take the time to remember my household and me in such intimate ways. Not all was perfect at home, but none of us could deny that God was real. This eagerness to share my testimony and do more for God's Kingdom made me feel restless at my church and after praying, I began to search for another church to attend.

One evening, I attended a political outdoor meeting in my neighborhood of Jackson, St. Michael. It was a Barbados Labour Party meeting. My eldest daughter Victoria and I accompanied a friend. As we were walking toward the main road in the direction of the meeting, a car flew past us at top speed. I said to my neighbor, "That car driving very fast!"

As we looked up the road, I saw the rim of the car's tyre, rolling, hitting the road, bouncing towards us just as fast as the car was being driven. I only had time to shout to my daughter, "Run, run Victoria, run to that church!" We were a stone's throw away from the entrance of Jackson Nazarene Church.

As I pushed Victoria out of the way I felt a strange presence on me, like a large hand pushing down my head and pressing me against the church's gate. Had I not ducked, the rim would have struck me on my head. The rim dropped into a gutter just in front of me.

The driver of the car came running to us, asking if anyone was hurt. We told him we were not touched but we were shaken up. My friend was so afraid; all she was saying was, "My God, look how I invited you out to a meeting and nearly caused you to be hurt."

Having lost interest in any political meeting, we all decided to head back home. While on our way, I confided in my friend, "Something strange happened to me just now, a strange presence came on me and pushed me out of harm's way and in the midst of the ordeal, I had a strong sense that I need to attend that Nazarene Church." I said nothing of it again that night, not even to my family. The next day, as I was taking the children to school, I saw that the doors of the Nazarene Church were open. The pastor of the church was inside the building. I wanted to talk to him but I was scared to approach him and introduce myself. Fear got the better of me and I went home. Later that evening, I prayed that God would show me how to approach the same pastor if He wanted me to do so. A few days passed, then the opportunity presented itself to me when I was returning home from taking the children to school. As I was passing the church, I saw the pastor doing work on the church building.

I walked over and greeted him in a mannerly tone. He responded in equal fashion and we started to have a friendly conversation. He told me his name was Pastor Bynoe. I looked at him and said, "I will be soon joining the church." He replied, "You are welcome." I felt warmth and love come from him as he spoke.

The Sunday, I took my children and a few others from the community to church. We were welcomed by the members and I felt like these people could become my new family.

Sunday after Sunday I eagerly attended services and the community children were just as eager to follow me. The warm reception we received made me all the more willing to say "yes" whenever a request was asked of me.

Within the Church of the Nazarene, elections are held every year for nominated officers to take up leadership positions within their respective local assemblies. When that time came around, Pastor Bynoe asked me to consider taking up the post of Sunday School president. I was shocked. "Not me! I now come!" I explained to him, thinking that no one in his right mind would vote for a woman who was not even a member for six months.

However, the pastor was able to convince me to give it a try and so I consented. Apparently, the church also had confidence in me because when the elections were through, I had received the majority of votes to head the Sunday School department. That evening of the elections, I said in my heart,

"Lord, You have proven tonight that man looks at the outward appearance, but You look at the heart. Here I am, a woman with nothing much, a woman who keeps a few pigs, a woman with no school certificates; yet you can use me. Amen."

Immediately, I got to work and with the help and cooperation of the members, more children attended church. Soon we had over fifty children. I planned Vacation Bible School programs, Church Harvest programs where the children would perform poems and songs. I planned Sunday School picnics and fun days for the children. My heart was devoted to serving the church and seeing these children impacted positively with the Good News of Jesus Christ. The influx of children did a lot to uplift the spirit of the church. I served in that capacity for the next five years.

Chapter 20
Favor at NCC

My babies were growing and becoming more independent. As I watched them develop, I yearned to move up in life as a woman. I yearned to be more independent, not having to depend on Guy for every single need that we had. My job as a domestic worker at the hotel was a temporary blessing. After that I had a few more temporary job offers, some were temporary because I was filling in for someone on vacation, but all had to be temporary because Guy was of the opinion that my place was in the home taking care of his children. He was not happy about me leaving the children with anyone else. However, this dependence on him caused him to financially abuse me (withhold finances from me or make me beg for money to take care of myself and the family), among other types of abuse, and it kept me in a vulnerable place as a woman.

At the beginning of 1999, a gentleman by the name of Mr. Neil came to the Nazarene Church and asked me if I wanted to work. Without blinking twice, I told him 'yes'. He agreed to assist me in securing a job at the National Conservation Commission (NCC). I remember praying to God and saying, "Father, I have kept your church in order and blessed you with everything I had, now I need you to bless me in 1999. I need a job, but please, no work in any sun."

An opportunity for a job interview presented itself to me. When I sat with an NCC manager and his assistant, he asked me what kind of job I was looking for. I remembered my prayer and I confidently told him that I wanted to be a ranger, working in the park. The manager looked at me and said, "The Lord truly sent you to me. These ranger positions have been closed, no more ranger job is available, but I will open a position for you." I thanked the man. It was the 2nd day of January, 1999. He asked me if I could work the following day and I said, "No." I had already planned a picnic for the Sunday school so I told him I would only be available to start from the Monday, the 4th of January. He agreed and we signed off on the work contract. Glory be to God!

My job started at Welchman Hall Park in St. Thomas, and then I was transferred to Harrison's Cave, not very far away. I passed my probationary period and the contract was extended. Favor rested on me and I got along with almost everyone. There was one ranger in particular that made it his business to let me know he did not like me very much. He would try to put blockages in my way and tell the other rangers that I was the manager's dog. When we were assigned to work together, he would arrive to work extremely late so that the bulk of the prep work needed to be done before the Cave was opened to the public, fell to me.

If I passed by him at a time when he was hanging out with the taxi drivers and other male rangers, he would shout at me, "Who let the dog out?" He would repeat it over and over again, trying to get a visible response out of me. I felt discouraged and insulted but I prayed to God that he would not let this man win over me.

I complained to the manager about the way this ranger was harassing me. The manager would say to me only that I was to remember who gave me the job and I was not to let any ranger run me away from what was mine.

I continued to work as onto God, embracing the opportunities to meet and greet people from all walks of life, tourists and locals alike. With every interaction, I became less conscious of the way I spoke. When I had something to say, I said it. My time there was a great training ground for learning how to handle people. I led Shawn Roberts to Christ while working at the Cave. We became good friends and she, along with her family, joined me at the church for fellowship.

Two years of working at Harrison's Cave passed by. I was then transferred to Farley Hill National Park. In my third year as an NCC ranger, the Government issued appointment letters for that particular post. Appointment means permanency, and we all were raised to believe that there was nothing more secure than a government job. I remember the day the letters came out; rangers were discussing among themselves who they felt would be or would not be appointed. I was told not to expect a letter because I had "just come on the job". The next day, I was summoned to go to the office. I confess I was shaking in my boots as I approached the supervisor.

He placed a brown envelope in my hand and said, "Congratulations!" I signed an acceptation letter and exited the office, being careful to walk away from where the other rangers were standing. Finding a tree, I sat down in solitude. I looked up to the sky and began to praise God, reminding Him of His promises to me. I remembered the manager saying to me when I first got my job, "Diana, don't worry, just do your work and do it honestly, I will do my part to make sure you have a job like anyone else, you work for God so I believe God will provide for you."

I opened the envelope and began to read the letter. It read that I had received the job appointment and it outlined details of a pension plan. Appointed! A pension plan? My God was hearing my cry. I jumped to my feet and shouted praises to God. I saw people staring but it did not move me. I heard people talking and questioning what was going on but it did not move me. Some even asked me how I could be appointed before others who had put in more years of work but that did not move me. I kept my mouth shut to them and directed whatever I had to say to God Almighty. Faithful God.

God used that experience to teach me about the verse in 1 Corinthians 1:27, "But God hath chosen the foolish things of the world to confound the wise; and God hath chosen the weak things of the world to confound the things which are mighty." God reminded me that He would use the simple Diana, who people saw as uneducated and unable to speak, to shock people in this very place and everywhere I would go.

Chapter 21
Dirty Hands

After some years as a member of the Jackson Nazarene Church, I made a decision to go back to my former church to assist Pastor Matthews in ministry. The church eventually had to be moved from off the land in St. George and it was relocated in St. Michael, about 10 minutes' drive away from my house. Pastor Matthews needed help and I always had a special place in my heart for him and his wife because of the integral role they played in my family, so I answered the call.

Pastor Matthews first called on me to work with the women of the church. I had been through so much already that I felt my experiences and how God brought me through them could help to encourage and empower the women. I wanted to teach them how to love God no matter what they might be going through. It did not go as well as I had planned and I found myself at the center of confusion and controversy.

One night, the pastor called some of the other women of the church and me into a meeting. I was accused of being too controlling and inserting myself where I was not welcomed. I was accused of wanting to come and change them with all my big ideas. It was hurtful to hear but I listened.

During the meeting I told the pastor I would step down from leading the women but he tried to dissuade me from doing so. However, the consensus was that I was not wanted in that position, so I bowed out. When the meeting concluded, I went home and with much tears, I asked the Lord, "Why have You allowed me to go back to that church? You knew the people would not want me." The Lord replied by bringing back to remembrance the verses in Isaiah 55: 8-9.

> *"For My thoughts are not your thoughts, Nor are your ways My ways," says the Lord. "For as the heavens are higher than the earth, So are My ways higher than your ways, And My thoughts than your thoughts."*

I encouraged myself that night and decided to stay and serve in whatever capacity opened to me.

Days after that, Pastor Matthews approached me once more, this time to lead the youth department. I jumped at the idea, believing that my years working with the Sunday school department at the Nazarene church would help me function in this role. I soon implemented Vacation Bible School and planned picnics and retreats for the youth. My passion was to see the young people grow in their faith and begin to see themselves as having worth, that they too could become powerful youth leaders. Oh how I enjoyed working and fellowshipping with them.

Revival time came around and the pastor brought in a minister from Trinidad and Tobago to preach during a week of revival services. During altar ministry on one of the evenings, this minister called me up to the front of the church and said to me that the Lord had been speaking to him concerning me. He began to say I was stubborn. I replied, "Okay, yes I know." He said, "It is not of bad, it is of good, there is a lot more God is showing me but I wouldn't say all of it right now." I nodded my head and returned to my seat.

For the remainder of the services, I positioned myself to assist in the altar work, comforting people after they were ministered to, sometimes praying with them and escorting them back to their seats.

One night in particular God revealed to me the reason behind the discomfort in my spirit about this foreign minister. The revelation played out in this manner. The minister called all of the young people to the altar for prayer. After he prayed for each of them, he sent them down to the basement of the church; this was where he stayed during his visit to Barbados. I continued to assist in the altar work when suddenly I heard a voice say to me, "Put someone else in your position, you need to go downstairs immediately." I could only conclude that this was God speaking to me, so I quickly obeyed. When I arrived downstairs, there in the basement I saw all of the young people rolling on the ground, squealing like pigs and crying out, "Help me! Help me!" My heart broke when I saw my youngest daughter Shelly-Ann rolling around on the ground and screaming for help. I looked up and saw three adults in the basement, they were praying over the children but they were not as alarmed as I was because they thought that the children were screaming under the power of the Holy Spirit. In fact, though the squealing and the screaming "help me" could be heard from upstairs, it seemed like the majority of people believed that this was the work of the Holy Spirit. So they just continued praying and shouting praises. How great the deception was!

At that moment, I felt the power from God rise up in me and words began to fly out of my mouth. I knelt down next to each child and in my believer's authority, commanded these demonic spirits oppressing the children, "Come out, you unclean spirit, I command you to go back in the name of Jesus Christ, I command you to loose [name of the child] and to return to your sender". When I reached over to where my daughter was lying, I saw that her eyes were closed and her body was rigid. I physically lay on top of my daughter, breathed into her mouth and commanded her to open her eyes. I prayed for her to be delivered from all unclean spirits until she was completely set free. All she was shouting was, "Mummy help me, please!"

As I prayed for some of the children, I asked God to cover them in the precious blood of His Son Jesus Christ and sent them back up the stairs. I then turned my attention to those who remained, pulled them apart as they were gripping each other and screaming. I prayed in the same manner for them to be delivered, asking God to cover them as I sent them back upstairs.

When I was finished praying, I went back to the area where the main service was being conducted. The Trinidadian pastor watched me intently; his staring eyes were like daggers. However, he said nothing to me.

The next day, my pastor approached me and told me how the minister told him that he needed to be careful with me and that there was much God had revealed to him about me but he chose not to say anything publicly to save me from being shamed.

His name was Minister Milton and he soon travelled back to his homeland, accompanied by my pastor whose intention was to minister at similar revival services with this man. I prayed and asked God to reveal who this man was to me, this man who dressed in white and told people the white represented the Glory of God, this man whose hands were dirty and who prayed over our young people, causing them to be bound.

Not long after their departure, I had a dream in which I saw Minister Milton and my pastor at the airport. Next to Minister Milton stood his four suitcases of varying sizes. I said to Minister Milton, "You have too many suitcases; you will have to pay for at least one." He was talking to my pastor at the time and he shouted across to me, "Okay, fix them for me."

I decided to put one of the smaller suitcases into a bigger one. When I opened the third suitcase, I saw two gloved hands reaching out to me; one was black and the other was white. I was so scared; I took some of the clothes that were in the suitcase, tried to cover and push down the hands but they would not lie down. I quickly sat on the suitcase to put enough pressure on it so that I could zip it up.

Minister Milton seemed not to notice my ordeal. Neither did the Pastor. Then I heard the Lord saying, "Witchcraft, that's what he was doing with his hands." As I got up from off of the suitcase, the dream ended.

I decided to call my pastor's wife to let her know about my dream. Nothing like this had happened to me before and at that time I was still unsure of who I was in God, unsure of his calling on my life, unsure of the spiritual gifts he had given me to function in His Kingdom. The pastor's wife was furious with me when she heard what I had to say. She shouted at me, "You lie, not my husband, Milton is going to carry him all over the place. Those hands you seeing are people raising their hands praising God. A lot of people will be worshipping God when they go around preaching." Confused, I said to her, "But Mother that is not what God said about the dream; the Lord told me that that man is working in witchcraft."

Our pastor stayed in Trinidad for one week. When he returned, his wife told him about the dream I shared with her and he requested to speak to me. We soon spoke over the telephone and I shared with him the contents of the dream. When I told him about the man's hands of witchcraft, my pastor told me, "looks like he got your hands then". I was hurt but I said nothing. The Lord said to me that the pastor would visit me soon.

After a few hours had passed, I saw my pastor at my door telling me he brought US$600 to sell me. I was preparing for an overseas trip and was asking around for anyone who had some US currency to sell. I used the opportunity to question him about his comment to me, that I had the same hands as the Trinidadian pastor. He said, "I was only joking." "Joking? Nothing about what you said was funny," I replied. My pastor started to tell me what had happened to him while he was in Trinidad. He recounted that as soon as both he and Minister Milton landed on the island and had passed through immigration, the minister walked ahead of the pastor, went through a door and was soon out of sight. My pastor spent hours looking for the man and waiting for him to return, but he did not. Luckily, my pastor had other contacts in Trinidad. He made contact with his former bishop and made inquiries into this minister. The bishop's report only served to confirm what the Lord had told me. The bishop revealed that this same minister had messed up people's lives under the guise of ministering to them. He was subsequently dismissed from that particular network of churches.

When my pastor asked why he was not warned about this rogue minister, the bishop responded that he would have been told if he had first asked a question. I said to him,

"Pastor, you could have caused the families in your church to be destroyed."

The consequences of his actions did not escape him. At a church meeting held to review the week of revival services, Pastor Matthews shared what had happened in Trinidad with Minister Milton, the report from the bishop, and the fact that he had had his own suspicions based on rumors but chose not to act on them.

Several members left. They could not overlook the danger under which they were placed by the pastor so they left the church. Others gradually followed. I believed God was angry and He was punishing the church for allowing itself to be so easily deceived.

Chapter 22
Evangelist Nicholls

After working with the youth of that Pentecostal church for a further two years, I felt it was time to move again and, on the invitation of a Christian friend, I went over to a New Testament Church of God assembly. This was yet another step in my preparation for ministry. I attended services for a year before being called on to do any type of service. One day the church had a revival and the pastor, Pastor Prince, called on me to pray for persons at the altar. I declined and refused to move from my seat that day. I said nothing aloud but in my heart I was fighting with God, "Not me, not me Lord. How could I lay my hands on someone to pray for them? Isn't that the pastors and ministers' duty? Besides that, I now come here. Why would she call on me to do something?" I did not know at that time what the pastor saw in me. I did what I knew to do well, run from the presence of God.

Sometime later, the church held a special revival service. A man came into the church for prayer and just at that time, my hands began to burn. I looked down at them to see that they had also turned red, as if all the blood in my body had rushed to them. I asked the pastor what was happening to my hands and in the process of me doing so, the man got up from his seat and approached the altar. My pastor looked at me and told me I had healing hands and that I was to lay my hands on the man. I was afraid but I obeyed the pastor and prayed for the man. While laying my hands on him, the man was delivered from his ailment. The people got up and came to the altar for prayer. A pastor from one of the New Testament Churches was among those persons. The Lord gave me a word of knowledge concerning him. He had cancer. I shared with him what the Lord told me and he confirmed it was true. As the Lord spoke to me I shared with the man, "The Lord is about to heal you right now, receive it in Jesus' name". Many people were healed that night.

During a Sunday service on another occasion, an old man attending suddenly fell on the ground as we were worshipping God in song. His daughter and family began to cry out. The ministers ran and laid their hands on him, calling for someone to bring sweets and alcohol. I heard the Lord saying to me, "Lay your hands on his face", so I did as the Holy Spirit instructed. As soon as I laid my hands on his face, the old man opened his eyes and started breathing. While my hands were on him, I felt a coldness come up from his head, up through my hands, then I felt heat in my hands go right through his face. The man stared up at me, eyes wide open.

I moved away while the ministers let him stand. While he was standing, he was still looking at me. I only told the pastor what had happened and she said, "That was God." The next Sunday, the pastor came to the church and told the ministers and members that the Lord spoke to her and from that day,

Sister Nicholls would no longer be referred to as Sister; her title would be changed to Evangelist. I opened my eyes, wanting to know what God was doing with me.

Some of the members questioned her, saying they were there at the church long before I started coming, yet she wanted to overlook them and call me Evangelist. She calmly replied, "The Lord said it and so it shall be."

My release into ministry shifted my spiritual gifts into a higher dimension and God used me more and more to minister to the lives of persons. I spent more time studying the Bible and eventually started writing out sermons secretly. One night the pastor approached me about preaching the Word of God. "You mean me preach? Me?" She looked at me and said, "Yes, those sermons that God has given you, use them". I did not tell her I had sermons; the only person that could have told her was God. The pastor saw a gift in my life that I was not able to see. She looked at me one day and said to me, "You are very special in God's sight."

Not long after that, my pastor asked me to preach as part of my training to becoming an Evangelist. She encouraged me to go to Bible College, stating that I needed to go deeper in the Word of God, and that without college training, I could not become ordained. Truthfully, I believed I would not be able to study well, much less commit to studying well for three years seeing that I was a school leaver without any certificates. So I declined.

As soon as I reached home from that particular meeting with Pastor Prince, I heard a voice come to me saying, "My daughter why are you doubting me? I have already sent the Holy Spirit with you who will teach you all things."

Chapter 23
I've made my Decision

That same year, 2005, my car collided with a truck, causing me to receive injuries to my back and neck. I was in excruciating pain but the Lord saw me through my ordeal.

On the day of the accident, I was reminded of an encounter I had with God a year earlier, on my way to Farley Hill Park. I had been battling heavy depression and suicidal thoughts. I had been reflecting on my personal life, that even though I was working in the church and being used by God in ministry, I still felt defeated at home. My marriage was a huge strain on my emotions. When I started to work, It was a hard task trying to stretch what I earned to cover food, bills and debt. Soon after I started working, Guy got a job working as a security guard for a government department. Even with this double income, I did not receive much money from him to run the household. Instead, I took what I earned and gave it to him to pay bills, which he seldom did. Our credit was in the red. Bailiffs came to our home on several occasion.

Then, there was the issue of the verbal and emotional abuse. Every time I seemed to be making progress in life, Guy would seek to pull the rug from under my feet. He would tell me I came from nothing, that he was the only one that could have me, that when he was finished with me, nobody else would want me. His wandering eye never left him, even though I kept hoping he would change after seeing all God had done for him and his family. One day, God gave me a prophetic word for him, which I shared with him. It was that even as his job was a blessing from God, it would be snatched away from him if he refused to honor his Creator and his family. Even after testifying how God had saved him in the truck accident and had caused him to walk again, even after that, Guy never truly repented from his wicked ways.

During that time in my life, I was vulnerable. I yearned to be loved by a man and would have gone wholeheartedly in the arms of those who were offering it to me, and a few were. However, for the sake of my children I could not leave.

I remember there was a man that would invite me out to parties to have fun and escape what was going on in my home. A few times, I went, and would tell my children to lie about my whereabouts if their father called home for me. These escapades were short-lived and I felt horrible for putting my children in that position. I stopped going out. It was home, work and church. The suicidal thoughts took up residence in my mind.

That very week I was driving on my way to work, a male friend of mine had won big in the lotto and had offered to give me $10, 000. Oh, what I could do for my family with $10, 000! I told him that I would accept the money. On that road to Farley Hill Park, I recall driving fast and as I was doing that, a voice told me, "Run the car off the road, kill yourself, just end your misery." I asked God to sit with me and help me reach to work safely. Suddenly, I heard the voice of God say to me as clear as day, "Diana, return to me and I will return to you. If you don't return to me I will take you home this very day." At that moment, I was driving through Content, St. Thomas. At His voice, I felt like a wretch lost in sin and totally at the mercy of God Almighty. I cried out in brokenness for God to save me and there, right there in that car, I committed my heart fully to God for Him to use me as He wanted. I told Him I would run from Him no more. I would sin no more. Coming out of that encounter, I called my friend and thanked him for the monetary offer but added that I could no longer accept it. Whatever friendships I had that would keep me one foot in the world, I cut off, and I committed myself to doing things God's way.

It was this encounter with God in 2004 that came forcefully back to my mind after my vehicular accident in 2005. The day after that accident, I called my pastor and told her that I wanted to go to college but I was afraid. I also told her I did not have the money to pay for tuition. Pastor Prince replied, "I think the doors are closed for anyone now who wants to enter college but I will still call the principal and ask a question."

The good Lord was truly on my side. The principal told her to let me come to her. I went to the college, picked up a form at the office and filled it out right there on the spot. I didn't have the down payment then but I had hope that God would provide it as it was His will for me to go to college and grow in Him.

I failed the entry examination but God favored me and I was allowed to retake it. When I returned to the school, the teacher clarified the instructions for me and gave me some pointers on how to approach the examination questions. I was able to pass the second time and started Bible College in September 2005.

My time at college was far better than I anticipated. I took each day as it came, rather than stare at the mountain of work before me. There was the issue of my speech. I would soak in the information presented but was so scared to speak in class. Every time we had an oral test, my heart would melt. However, the teachers were supportive.

My first year was very challenging for me, I had to research the church's history using the internet, newspapers, the Bible, resource books, you name it. My biggest challenge was reading but I was determined. I began to go deep down in the Bible for the word to help me. Every year my mind got deeper and stronger in the Word of God. Whenever I did my research, I found that I would go so deep and write so much, until one day my principal Dr. Joseph, looked at me and said, "Do you know Diana? You are going to write books." I smiled and said to myself, "She doesn't know what she's talking about."

My job as a park ranger gave me the time to be able to go to college and manage the workload, so did my job as a mother. Looking back, I could not have achieved what I did without that support system around me. I recall especially how my daughter Christine would go to sleep late many nights, helping me do research and study for my exams.

Chapter 24
House Divided

After the first year of college, another set of darts came at me with full force to destroy my faith. Firstly, I dreamt that Guy was having an extra-marital affair with another woman. I knew he was unfaithful to me before but I decided to confront him. When I did, he told me that the dream was true. Not long after, a woman who knew both of us, and who knew about Guy's new mistress, contacted me and told me what she knew of the affair. She also advised that both Guy and I should be tested for HIV. I recall how my thoughts went straight to the worst-case scenario. "Oh God, this is going to stop me from studying!" I thought, my chest tightening from anxiety.

The morning we went to be tested, I was a huge ball of nerves on edge, a nervous breakdown waiting to happen. Oh God what would I do if we tested positive? I knew God could heal all diseases but my faith was under real pressure and I could not even pray for myself. It so happened that the doctor who tested us was a believer. I was tested first, then Guy. While in his office, the doctor told me, "I do not call people to tell them anything on the phone; they have to come in to see me for their results".

In that time of waiting, I could not function at work, home, school or church. My head started to hurt me so badly that I thought, if not AIDS, surely this pain would kill me. I confided in no one because I felt I could not share such a thing without bringing shame on my family and myself.

Some days later, while at work, I sat down under a tree in solitude and cried out to God. "Please save me, please deliver me; if You do, I will never look back, and I will serve You all the days of my life." I was wavering in my faith and was overcome with grief and sorrow but I heard Him say to me through the Holy Scriptures, Romans 8:37-39,

> *Yet in all these things we are more than conquerors through Him who loved us. For I am persuaded that neither death nor life, nor angels nor principalities nor powers, nor things present nor things to come, nor height nor depth, nor any other created thing, shall be able to separate us from the love of God which is in Christ Jesus our Lord.*

I began to look to the heavens and praise God for His comfort. I said to God, "Lord, let me ask You to do one more thing for me, please. The doctor said he doesn't call anyone, but allow him to call me. Show me this thing, as a sign that you have delivered me once more."

That evening I went to classes at the college. I had a surprisingly profound peace upon me that allowed me to focus on what was going on around me.

During the class, my phone rang. It was the doctor calling me. I took the call outside of the classroom. He began to say to me, "My dear, I don't call anyone, but the Holy Spirit told me to call you". I listened. My heart felt like it had stopped beating. "…the result of your HIV test is negative…" he continued. Without thinking, I shouted, "Thank you Jesus, thank you doctor!" I am sure the entire school heard me. The doctor went on to encourage me to protect myself sexually and not to take life for granted. As he hung up, I began to cry. Rivers of tears streamed down my face. All I could do was declare, "Thank you Jesus! Thank you Jesus!"

Eventually, I returned to class, more confident that nothing would stop me from doing what I went there to do.

When I returned home that evening, I held a meeting with my husband and children. I explained to the children in particular that their parents needed a separation because their father's behavior was putting my life and health at risk. By then, the children were old enough to understand the dynamics of our turbulent relationship over the years. Our separation came as no surprise to them because we had always practiced inclusive discussion on the important things in our family. Despite the separation, and despite Guy continuing to pursue his love interests elsewhere, he did everything in his power to stop me from studying.

The darts continued, this time in the form of a vehicular accident in 2008. As in 2005, this accident was as a result of a car crashing into my own. The devil was truly out to hinder me, even take my life. The impact of the car crash affected my back and neck. The pain was so debilitating in the days and weeks that followed that I had to receive out-patient treatment at a clinic. When that did not work, I moved from doctor to doctor to receive therapy. My body would not respond to the medication and I continued to be in pain. I was eventually sent to the hospital for an MRI, which pointed to sustained injuries to my back.

The pain made it impossible for me to go out to work. I could not even dress myself or sit on the toilet for extended periods. To get off my bed was gigantic task. I began to think that if my time on the earth was running out, I needed to hastily complete the assignment God had given to me. I used that time at home to plant myself deep in God's word, to be sure of what He was saying to me. As I reflected on what I learned in Bible College and on what was spoken over my life by my teachers, I had no doubt that God wanted to use me more to work in His Church.

In 2008, with the help of God, I was able to pass all of my Bible College exams. Many were the afflictions on my way to achieving this. The Lord saw me through every one of them.

Chapter 25
Call to the Pastoral Ministry

In 2009, God sent people my way to confirm His calling on my life for the pastoral ministry. It had been prophesied to me in my last weeks at Bible College that my calling was to this ministry. Dr. Joseph, the principal of the College, declared to me, "You will be a pastor and quickly it will come to pass". I remember looking at her and saying, "Not me ma'am, I cannot be a pastor, I can't handle being a pastor. First of all, I cannot talk, so how will I be able to teach people?

Ma'am, you sure your heard clearly from God?"

Yet, my evaluations were revealing that my strongest spiritual gifts were exhortation, evangelism and shepherding. The principal explained that those gifts put me in an ideal position to handle pastoral duties. The principal said to me, "Diana, before I close my eyes, you will be a pastor and listen to me, my daughter, you will not only be a pastor, but you have been called into a higher realm."

I was now an ordained Evangelist at United Holiness Church of Faith in Christ, in St. Thomas. I also ministered at various churches across the island. I would preach the Word of God, prophesying as the Holy Spirit led and I would see many persons healed from various ailments.

But being responsible for God's flock scared everything out of me. All I could see were my shortcomings. When my doubt was greatest, the Lord would remind me of the story of Moses, of the assignment on his own life and all the miracles God used him to perform among the nation of Israel. Moses doubted himself incapable of completing his assignment at first, so he did not want to do it. Just like me, fear had him believing that the people would not believe him, that they would accuse him of lying about the Lord appearing to him. Moses said to God in Exodus 4:10,

> *"O my Lord, I am not eloquent, neither before nor since You have spoken to Your servant; but I am slow of speech and slow of tongue."*

But the Lord questioned Moses in verses 11 and 12, *"Who has made man's mouth? Or who makes the mute, the deaf, the seeing, or the blind? Have not I, the Lord? Now therefore, go, and I will be with your mouth and teach you what you shall say."*

I reflected on how as a little girl, I would beg God to take away my slow speech so that my mother would love me, so that the children would not tease me and call me Dummy Diana. I truly believed it was not too hard a task for Him to do. Yet, God never answered. Now, here He was, through His Word, asking me, "Who has made man's mouth? Or who makes the mute?" Like Moses, I had spent so much time begging Him and my pastors, "Please send someone else", someone I felt was more articulate, was more intelligent and was more fit to be used by

God. No matter how Moses, tried, he could not escape what God had for Him to do, and so too, I could not run from God. I had to trust him to use all of me, including my heavy tongue, to get the job done.

A particular day, pain came over my body such that I could not get out of bed. A friend came by to visit me and said he was on his way home from work when the Holy Spirit told him to come see me. Seeing my condition, he began to pray for me as I lay there in my bed. He then said to me, "Hear the word of the Lord. The Lord says to tell you, He is calling you into a higher level of ministry and you cannot say 'no' or turn away from it. He says you are called into the pastoral; someone is going to send for you to place you as a pastor. He says you are not to look back at negative words that will be spoken over your life; He already removed them. He says He will come to you in a vision and show you the way; he said the mission is an emergency and you need to accept it." I was not able to speak to my friend, only listen to what he was saying to me. After he prayed, he then left me on my bed speaking in tongues.

In the still of the night, the Lord appeared to me in a vision: *January 2009 - I was driving my car and Crystal, my daughter, was with me. She had an upset stomach so I stopped the car and allowed her to get out. As she was standing outside of the car, I told her I was going to leave her if she took too long to get back inside. I went to put the car into drive. Instead, the gear shifted to reverse and the car reversed itself until it got to the graveyard in St. Andrew Parish Church. All my attempts to stop the car failed.*

The car eventually parked itself along the road by the graveyard. I saw graves begin to open up and dead people begin to crawl out of these graves. They then walked towards me. I also saw a cat, dog, rat and all other kinds of animals come up from under the earth. The dead then flew on me, along with the animals. They were trying to tear off my skin but no matter how hard they tried, they could not succeed. Then the dead pressed up against me and tried to eat up my flesh. But no matter how hard they tried, they could not succeed.

Afterward, I looked up to the sky. There, a big, black image flew over me, saying, "I sent my people to destroy you and you would not die, well, I came myself and will do it; I am the head." I was not afraid of the being and shouted at it. I could not see its eyes, only all black. I said, "You can get my body but you cannot get my soul, I already gave it to Jesus Christ, I am already sold out to my savior!"

I began to shout out the name of Jesus Christ, over and over again, at each mention of the Name of Jesus Christ, the ghastly being backed away from me, eventually flying upward into the air and then disappearing. When it was gone, I saw the dead move away from the car and walk right back into their coffins. The coffins closed and the soil refilled the graves until all was normal again. The animals too disappeared underground. I tried starting the car to drive off but it would not cooperate, so I jumped out of the vehicle and ran as fast as I could.

While running, I saw my bishop. He was close to a church with a rake on his shoulder walking. I looked at him but did not stop running because I wanted to get back to Crystal. Next, I saw the pastor of the same church and the evangelist sweeping the road for me to pass by but I did not stop.

After I passed them, I continued to run. I soon came to the wife of a leading political figure of the nation at that time. She sat by the gates of St. Andrew Primary School and presented her two children to me. I continued by, in an effort to reconnect with Crystal. Soon I approached the road leading to my childhood neighborhood. Suddenly, a tall, dark man with a Bible tucked under one arm, smiled welcomingly at me and reached out a hand toward me. He said to me, "I was here waiting on you, come, let's go," he held my hand and I awoke from my vision.

I questioned God about this vision over the next year or so as elements of it began to play out in my life. Days after Guy called me and told me some people wanted to talk to me. He told me that one was the bishop of a local church and two other men were his work colleagues. He did not say why they wanted to speak with me. I agreed to meet them.

Not long after, the men came over to our family home. Guy was present and introduced them to me. Bishop Herbert was tall and of dark complexion. Immediately, I sensed this was the same man who appeared to me in the vision, took my hand and bid me to go with him. When everyone was comfortable, the men wasted no time making clear the purpose of their visit. They told me that God had sent them to me to "bring me into pastoral duties" and that "the Lord was calling me to be a pastor". They told me, "This time you cannot run, you cannot say 'no' to God anymore, He will not take 'no' for an answer."

Bishop Herbert and his two ministerial colleagues continued by saying that I had a special and specific assignment from God, that God had not revealed it all to them but that it would surpass being a local pastor. As I reflected on this, my stomach felt like it was doing somersaults. I was hearing what was being said to me, I was right there in the room and yet I felt as if I was on the outside, looking in, a witness to someone else's life purpose being unraveled. They said "special" and "specific". What would be special and specific about the assignment God was giving to me? Was this the reason why the dead and decaying were trying to kill me, that the darkness of the air was trying to eat my flesh? Ephesians 6:12 -13 says,

> *For we do not wrestle against flesh and blood, but against principalities, against powers, against the rulers of the darkness of this age, against spiritual hosts of wickedness in the heavenly places. Therefore take up the whole armor of God, that you may be able to withstand in the evil day, and having done all, to stand.*

What specifically was God calling me to stand against? What was I to stand for? I still had many questions, why was I separated from Crystal? Why were those who spoke against me or who allowed persons to sway their opinion of me through idle gossip sweeping the way for me to pass by? I told the men I would prayerfully consider all they told me and would get back to them with an answer.

That night I was not able to sleep. I went to the church the following night with my heart troubled, troubled like I had done something sinful, troubled like I had the world on my shoulders. In my heart, I asked God to help me and make clear the way before me. After the service, a friend and fellow worker in the ministry, Deacon Springer came to me and said, "Go. Go, the Lord has already opened the door for you… answer the calling." He told me, "Diana, God already spoke to me and told me not to stop you."

Peace came over me like a warm blanket. I felt God's presence begin to loosen the uneasiness inside of me.

When Bishop Herbert returned to my house to see if I had made up my mind, I said to him, "Yes, I will accept the calling." I wrote my resignation letter and gave it to the overseer of my church.

On January 22nd 2009, I was ordained a Reverend at Pray and Worship Ministry and received my certificate of ordination from Trinity Christian Tabernacle International in Trinidad and Pray and Worship Ministry Barbados.

I worked at the church and helped to build it up. I also went around to different churches around the island ministering the Word of God. Doors opened for me also to preach the gospel in Trinidad and Tobago. There, God used me to prophesy to church leaders and ministers. The Holy Spirit moved powerfully in those services. People were healed. People were set free. As I abandoned myself to God, my frail humanity was no longer an issue. Rather I saw that God could use anyone tremendously once he or she availed oneself to Him. God does not call the qualified. He qualifies the called. And I was called by God.

Chapter 26
United Family of Praise

I continued to serve the church faithfully at Pray and Worship Ministry, under the leadership of Bishop Herbert and his wife. God had been so gracious to me up to this point and I was not looking for any further shifting for a little while. On the home front, I was encouraged by my leadership to work on restoring my marriage to Guy. We were still living under the same roof but shared no intimacy as man and wife since our agreement to separate. This was seen as a "questionable area" in my ministry and so Bishop Herbert agreed to counsel us.

I was also still working at the NCC, despite ongoing pains from the accident in 2008. My children were young adults. Victoria was a trained police officer, Crystal was at college pursuing commercial studies, Christine and my youngest daughter Shelly were settling down in the world of work.

One day, the bishop's wife approached me and told me that God had been speaking to her about me. She told me, "Diana, there is more", then shared two dreams concerning this "more" to which she referred.

In the first, she recounted how I had been adorning the church in gold, white and purple dressing in anticipation of an upcoming worship service. On top of the altar, she recalled seeing two large eagles, perched on both sides. The bishop's wife said that the décor, including the eagles, could be clearly seen from the entrance, but that no one was able to enter the church on the day of the service. She then said that bishop came to check up on what I was doing. She opened the church door for him to see but even he could not step foot into the church. He enquired about the presence of the eagles and, when told that I had placed them on the altar, turned around and walked away in the direction of his home.

In the second dream, Mother Herbert was preparing for me to get married. She recounted that she was the one dressing all the tables for the reception. She said, "I was able to find table cloths to fit all of the tables in the reception hall, except for the head table for the bride and bride groom. All of the cloths I tried to put on had stains and were too short to cover the table properly. All how I looked, I could not find any… and I woke up from the dream."

I pondered on all that was shared with me. I was excited and fearful, curious but still wanting to remain in what was becoming my new comfort zone. But God had different ideas.

On 24th October 2009, I was involved in another vehicular accident. I had not fully recovered from the accident in 2008, so this one, though not damaging the car as seriously as the year before, unraveled whatever recovery I had managed to achieve through therapy. All I could do was cry out in pain and frustration. The pain and the frequent medical appointments that came along with it led to my attendance at work becoming sporadic at best. I had to receive a series of steroid injections to my spine to minimize the pain. Eventually, I was released from NCC duty, being declared "medically unfit" to work by a medical board. This was another major setback for my family and me. Nevertheless, I could still hold my head up high at the mark I made while serving my country under the NCC. I was a finalist in several employees' incentive program awards for *Customer Service*, as well as for *Efficiency and Productivity*.

The next few months, I tried to make sense of what was happening in my life. Naturally, I had some doubts about getting by without working. I still had bills and loans to take care of. What could I possibly do in the meantime, considering the state of my back?

One day, God answered, albeit differently to what I would have conceived. I was sitting at home and I heard the Lord say to me, "My daughter, I am calling you to handle my work in a divine authority; you are to write this name down." I got up immediately from where I was sitting to fetch a pen and some paper. I then heard, "Write 'United Family of Praise'", and I obeyed, even though nothing else was said to give me insight into what those words were supposed to mean to me. I then saved the name on my computer.

Months passed.

I continued to serve God faithfully, even when challenges arose in the ministry, as will happen in any ministry once people are involved. I reminded myself that I needed to give my all for God or nothing. He would not accept me being in between, being a lukewarm, compromising servant.

One day, I was before the Lord in prayer and He told me to look for somewhere to build His church that He had told me about. Stunned, I asked God, "What church did You tell me about? You never told me such a thing!" Memories began to flood my mind about the time, months before, when He had told me to write down a name He would give me. Did I hear God correctly? I was unsure and needed confirmation. I called my first pastor, Pastor Matthews, to see if God had spoken to him and given him a word for me, like Samuel and Eli, when God was calling Samuel into his divine calling and he did not understand his voice.

Pastor Matthews said to me, "If the Lord spoke to you answer his call." I said to him, "No, I rather stay at home or go by any church." He said, "The Lord have a church for you to take care of, do not leave your current position until you answer the calling that the Lord is placing in your heart." I said to him, "Okay, I will pray and fast about it."

One day a Sister in the Lord, Sister Collymore, called me and said the Lord had given her a dream about me. I told her, "Tell me." She told me that she saw me with a beautiful church. I replied, "Oh okay, where?" She said, "Under your house, it was so beautiful and fixed with the finest things, and I was also leading worship."

"What church? Who told you about a church?" I asked her, my heart was racing as I wondered who told her. Did Pastor Matthews break my confidence? She shouted, "Pastor Diana, I heard it from God!"

Our conversation soon ended. I decided to go before God about what Sister Collymore had said to me. "God, what are you saying to me? Do you really want me to build a church under my home?" I earnestly asked Him. Then, I recalled the New Testament accounts of various men and women, believers who opened their homes to have fellowship. Then I thought, what is church if not fellowship with God and with his children?

Church in my basement! I began to laugh as I warmed up to the idea. Who would imagine? Our family 'basement' was underdeveloped space under our house where rejected piglets were kept and nourished. It was a farm nursery of sorts. I would bring the piglets inside and nurse them milk with from a bottle. They were rejected by their mothers but in that basement, they were taken care of, they had rest. Ha! A church in the basement. Who would have thought?

With much thought and even more prayer, I decided to take God at His word. I approached some people about joining with me to start fellowship services and help me build a new church. I approached people I knew from church, from work, friends and folks from my community. Several agreed to join me.

Guy helped me to refurbish the space, section by section, including toilets. We built an altar and a platform, as well as steps allowing persons to more easily enter the basement. We then painted the room and installed electrical fans. I purchased musical instruments, microphones and speakers, very excited to give God the best I could give to His service and His people. Preparing the Church's constitution was not as straightforward. However, Pastor Matthews, who by this time was ordained as a church bishop, provided me with much needed assistance. In two months I had a satisfactory, official document which was eventually approved by the Corporate Affairs Intellectual Property Office.

United Family of Praise in Christ Mission Assembly. That was the official name of the church on the document. But I knew the work ahead would entail much more than a document in my hand. Just like a first-time mother with a new-born baby, I was nervous about making sure I did things the right way and that I heard from God correctly. Just as friends and family members can all have their varying views on how best to raise your child, I was bombarded with ideas, bits of advice and even reminders of what I could not do or was not equipped enough to do. But I sensed God with me during this time, His hand of order guided my decision-making and helped me to stand firmly on His word. I drew counsel from St. Paul's instructions to Timothy and Titus as young leaders and elders in churches. This would not be my first time pastoring, but for the first time, I would pastor an independent church. I would have to face many faces, faces of large giants in the Christian service, many of them males, some extending a hand to help, some doubting, even denying God's call on my life.

On March 19th, 2010, Bishop G. Webster dedicated the church and I was ordained as its pastor. Our services began with 30 members and as the Word of God was preached, believers were added to the Body of Christ.

Dressed in my ordination gown, I could not help but to stand back and see the handiwork of God all over my life. I remembered the little girl from Belleplaine St. Andrew, the one they all called **Dummy Diana**. I was the one who would cry tears upon tears, wanting God to heal me from my speaking disability. God did not answer me how I had hoped. In fact, it seemed sometimes that God was nowhere to be found. Neither did God heal my marriage to Guy as I would have hoped. Despite counseling, we simply could not live in agreement and would eventually divorce. Guy also lost the very job God had blessed him with for 14 years, according to the prophetic word God had used me to release to him. He received no severance pay nor benefits of any kind because he had failed to honor his Creator and his family.

Dressed in my ordination gown, I could not help but appreciate the path God would take this little, heavy-tongue stutterer from a rural village in Barbados. Rugged coast-lines battered relentlessly by elements beyond my control, sprayed with salt which burns but also purifies, I would not have chosen this path for myself. But God, who created me for Him, lifted me from the dust of hardship and filled my mouth with power to preach to the nations.

As I received my license of pastoral ministry, I smiled. "Ha! Only God could have done this", I said to myself. "Choose a *dummy* to shout from the roof top!"

And that is what I intend to do for the rest of my life. My mission is to declare God's message, not as a dummy, but as a daughter of God, called and qualified by Him. I will not be silent for anyone. With this voice, I will be heard!

To the Reader

I wrote this book to let you know that whoever you are, wherever you are in life, you are someone important. In fact, you are so important to the universe that God would have thought it incomplete without you. And that is why He made you. God's handprint on your life will not automatically exclude you from troubles and hardship, from sorrow and ill-treatment, from lack and loneliness. It means however, that He will keep His promise to see you through every storm, every shadowy valley, every scorching midday, if you will let Him. You are His own. You are special.

When I reflect on my life and see what God has done for me, where He has brought me from, I can only conclude with the psalmist that I must,

> *Bless the Lord, O my soul,*
> *And forget not all His benefits:*
> *Who forgives all your iniquities,*
> *Who heals all your diseases,*
> *Who redeems your life from destruction,*
> *Who crowns you with lovingkindness and tender mercies,*
> *Who satisfies your mouth with good things, So that your youth is renewed like the eagle's.*
>
> **(Psalms 103: 1-5)**

Oh hallelujah!

You may be saying that you are nothing. You may see yourself as an insignificant person in your family, church or place of work. "Oh, I am least educated... oh, I've been doing the same job for the past twenty years... oh, don't call on me to pray, I'm just the janitor!" you keep crying. Listen to me readers, when there is a divine assignment attached to your life, the devil knows and he will try all sorts of ways to delay, deny and destroy you. People can love you one minute, then turn their backs on you the next. Your own family can reject you. Be encouraged! That assignment that God has given you must be fulfilled, even at the midnight hour! Sister, don't run! Brother, you can't hide any longer. There is a mission before you and your life is the key to executing it.

To those of you who may be experiencing marital trials, I make it clear that I am not a believer in divorce (despite my experiences shared in this book. Use all the tools of reconciliation at your disposal. Use prayer, Spirit-led communication, pastoral and marital counseling, even temporary separation should your case warrant it. Above all, let your life be your greatness witness to your spouse, by cultivating daily the fruit of the Spirit (Galatians 5:22-23). May the Lord come through for you in your marriage! Still, if an unbelieving spouse wishes to go his or her own way, you cannot force that person to do otherwise. God calls us to live in peace. (1Corinthians 7:15)

Do not let regret or condemnation or thoughts of failure paralyze you. The truth that the enemy wants to keep from you is that you can move from where you are. Yes! The only location that is final in this lifetime is the grave. If you are not there yet, it means you can move up and move on in the Lord, in the authority that God has already given you. Believe it with me today. God is about to take you to a higher level.

Do not shut up or shut down for anyone. Tell the devil "Ain't no dummy around here!"

Loving you through to victory,
Apostle Diana A. Nicholls

www.ingramcontent.com/pod-product-compliance
Lightning Source LLC
Chambersburg PA
CBHW072154160426
43197CB00012B/2383